DILLON

HOW TO MAKE BIG MONEY SELLING

HOW TO MAKE BIG MONEY SELLING

By Joe Gandolfo

with Robert L. Shook

HARPER & ROW, PUBLISHERS, New York

Cambridge, Philadelphia, San Francisco, London

1817 *Mexico City, São Paulo, Singapore, Sydney*

FIRST EDITION

Designer: Sidney Feinberg

Library of Congress Cataloging in Publication Data

Gandolfo, Joe, 1936–
   How to make big money selling.

    1. Selling.   I. Shook, Robert L.   II. Title.
HF543825.G36   1984   658.8'5   84-47569
ISBN 0-06-015324-5

---

84 85 86 87 88 10 9 8 7 6 5 4 3 2 1

To Carol, my beloved wife, for all her patience.

To Irv Levey, my editor.

It is impossible to meet each reader in person, but I hope through these words we have met.

Contents

Introduction

BY ROBERT L. SHOOK

How would you like to spend a few evenings with the world's best salesperson, just picking his brains?

Well, I've spent a lot of time during the past several months with Joe Gandolfo, asking every question I could come up with; and to me Joe is a hero with the stature of a Babe Ruth or a Sergeant York. Although I'm a full-time writer now, I spent seventeen years selling insurance: first as an agent, then as a general agent, and still later as the chairman of a life insurance company. So I have long known about the Gandolfo legend in the business. I wanted to find out how a single life insurance agent could sell $800 million of life insurance year after year; and if he really did sell more than $1 billion of life insurance in 1976! In an industry that makes a big fuss over salespeople who sell a million each year, Joe's production exceeds most insurance companies' annual sales volume.

When I wrote the book, *Ten Greatest Salespersons*, I

chose only those individuals who were number one in their respective fields. In researching that book, I discovered that Joe was not only the world's leading insurance agent, but perhaps the highest-paid salesperson ever. So, when he asked me to help him with this book, I accepted with delight. It was the ideal assignment for me, a salesperson-turned-writer.

When we first began this book, Joe agreed to tell the hows and whys of his remarkable success in a way that would help any salesperson in *any* field. Above all we wanted a book that would clearly show how *enormous* earnings can be made in sales: annual incomes that could far exceed those of the highest-paid professionals!

So, this book is primarily for the very ambitious, those who want to set company and industry sales records. If you have read many books about selling, you're going to be surprised to find Joe's philosophy and selling techniques so unorthodox and unique. He accepts the idea that a successful person may reach his level by learning all the rules and following them to the letter, but to be a super-successful person, Joe says you must learn all the rules and then rewrite them. To those who view Joe's methods with raised eyebrows, I say, "Look at his record. Unless you are already a superstar, you should seriously consider alternatives to your old ways."

When I first began talking to friends about Joe, they questioned his record year. "Come on, Bob. You don't really expect anyone to believe that one agent could sell a billion dollars of life insurance in a single year? Aren't you stretching it just a little?"

"He really did it," I'd insist. Then I'd go through a

long explanation about my research to verify his sales records.

When I mentioned to Joe how much flak these people were giving me, he said, "Just tell them the only thing that needs stretching is their minds." Somehow, when I'm around Joe Gandolfo I get the feeling that anything is possible. He likes to quote great sports personalities, but one of his favorite quotes is from Napoleon Hill's best-selling book *Think and Grow Rich:* "Whatever the mind of man can conceive and believe, it can achieve."

"I live by those words," Joe says; and I'm sure he means it.

A speaker in much demand, Joe tells his audience, "Every human being needs to dream and should strive to turn those dreams into reality. This can be accomplished if you have enough faith in God and yourself, apply self-discipline, and are willing to make the necessary sacrifices. In my case, I was also helped by an understanding and loving spouse."

Joe grew up in the small town of Richmond, Kentucky. His father had migrated to the United States; and a few years later, Joe's mother, the oldest daughter of a Sicilian farmer, was brought over for an arranged marriage. Joe's parents had never met each other until the day of their wedding. They settled in Richmond, where his father tried his hand in many business ventures, including ice cream, liquor, and real estate. Still later, he owned a Packard-Kaiser-Frazer dealership with a younger brother. "My father was a hardworking man," Joe says proudly, "who always preached that you can do whatever you want in America, but the best thing is to be in business for yourself. Those words have always stayed with me." And, as an independent insurance agent, Joe is in business for himself, as he has been practically all of his career as a salesperson. Today he runs a business that nets millions of dollars each year.

Joe's strong faith in God stems from his mother's deep religious beliefs. Throughout his early childhood, she took him to early Mass every morning. When he was only twelve, she died of cancer at the age of thirty-nine. Tears still come to his eyes when he speaks about her. After her death, Joe was sent away to Kentucky Military Institute where he tells about often crying himself to sleep, "because I missed her so much." During his senior year, his father had a fatal heart attack. From this point on, Joe's life was excruciatingly lonely. His father's brother was appointed guardian and named executor of the estate. Joe's older sister and two younger brothers were sent off to live with out-of-state relatives, and it wasn't until Joe was twenty-six years old that he saw them again. His father died without a will, and his uncle took everything from the four children, although the court did make provisions for their education.

He describes his loneliness as having been unbearably painful. His memory of his parents is that they were a loving and affectionate couple. They were hardworking people; God always came first in their lives; and the family was second. Their work was third. "Even though their days were long, they always had time for us children. We were hugged and kissed and loved."

After their deaths, Joe says it was his belief in God that carried him through this difficult period of his life.

"I decided to turn my life over to Him. I simply said, 'God, do with me what you will and I am willing to accept it.' Once I could unconditionally accept God's will, I could live with my loneliness. God became my partner and strength."

Joe credits his days at military school for his complete self-discipline. Kentucky Military Institute enforced a strict code of behavior, and as Joe puts it, "It was like being in continuous army basic training as a teenager." Joe enjoyed the strictness—even the daily drilling, the inspections, and the rigid punishment he had to face for stepping out of line.

At KMI, Joe devoted his energies to his studies and to sports, always being a familiar face in the study hall and on the practice fields. He had a burning desire to excel at whatever he participated in, whether it was collecting the most baseball cards, seeing the most movies, or being the toughest kid. He had to be number one. "My secret for being the best was quite simple," he confesses. "I was willing to work harder than anyone else to get what I wanted. Most people aren't willing to pay the price."

By his senior year, he was the school's star quarterback, a baseball standout, and Number One Cadet with a straight-A average. After his graduation in 1954, Joe went to Vanderbilt, a school not known for a winning tradition in sports, but where he played baseball, his first love. Dissatisfied with the school's sports program, he transferred to Miami of Ohio, where he majored in mathematics and played on Miami's baseball team.

His college days at Miami were happy. He made good grades, played good baseball, and for the first time in his life, had "a normal social life." He never lacked for girl friends. "I dated all the campus beauties," he says "and not because of my good looks. But because I had a hunch that they were lonely! The other guys presumed that those girls would always be dated up, so they never asked them for dates. Not me. I called them and found out they were lonely.

"It taught me a good lesson that I have applied throughout my sales career. I never assume that the most affluent people or the biggest accounts have already been sold—like those college guys with the campus beauties. I've always made it a point to call on the biggest people. It's easier to sell a $5 million policy to a multimillionaire than it is to sell a $50,000 policy to a man making $25,000 a year. And, selling one $5 million policy produces a hundred times greater volume and commissions!"

In a biology class, there was one particular student that caught Joe's eye—Carol Lorentz, a slim, beautiful blonde. He couldn't take his eyes off her. One day the professor asked for someone to remove his shirt so a heart could be diagrammed on his chest; and since Carol was sitting in the front row, Joe volunteered. While the professor painted away, Joe asked Carol for a date. She turned him down. For three months he pursued her and was continually rejected. Finally, a friend who dated Carol's roommate set up a double date. Joe's persistence paid off. It took his all-time-best selling efforts, but he finally made the sale. He has never dated another woman.

Joe was graduated in 1958; and that summer he went to Cincinnati, where he played professional baseball. By the end of the summer he and Carol were engaged, and they were married on December 26.

While he loved playing baseball, he despised the road trips. "I didn't drink, smoke, or cuss like so many of my teammates; and I couldn't stand sleeping in dingy hotels. I just didn't fit in," he tells.

By 1959, Joe got baseball out of his system, and he and Carol moved to Fort Lauderdale, Florida, where he took a job as a math teacher and part-time coach. He earned $238 a month. Their son, Michael, was born in 1960, and soon Carol was expecting a second child. Even in those days, $56 a week didn't do much more than put food on the table, so when a life insurance company contacted Joe to discuss a sales career, he went to see what they had to offer. It was a company that had sold him a policy while he was at Miami University, and they wanted him to sell life insurance to college students.

He took the company's aptitude test and barely passed. It was agreed that if he could sell ten policies, or $100,000 of insurance in the next ninety days, they'd give him a guarantee of $450 a month. "I'm a math teacher and an ex-jock," he told Carol, "not a salesman."

"What do you have to lose?" she replied. "You can always go back to teaching."

During the summer of 1960, he studied and memorized a twenty-two-page sales presentation given to him by College Life Insurance Company. He practiced with Carol day and night; and by the time he was ready to start his actual in-the-field selling, he knew it cold.

He planned to work for ninety days in Baton Rouge, Louisiana, a city of 200,000 where he didn't know a single person. He would call on college seniors at Louisiana State University and on young people like him just entering the job market. His first sale was on his own life—the twenty-two-page sales presentation sold him!

It was agreed that Carol would spend the next ninety days with her parents in Portsmouth, Ohio, and have their second child there. Joe's plan was to work seven days a week, putting in ninety to a hundred hours. "I was going to give it my best shot," he explains. "I was willing to do everything exactly as the company taught me, and not deviate from their training one iota. If the company managers were right, then I'd be successful. If they were wrong and I failed, it would be their fault, not mine."

He rented a small room in a policeman's home for thirty-five dollars a month. His first night, he recalls getting down on his knees and praying to God for hours asking for his support. By noon the next day, he made seven appointments and thought selling was going to be "a piece of cake." But he discovered that completing a sale was a lot tougher than getting in to see a prospect. He struck out seven times that first day—having nothing to show for sixteen hours of selling! He punished himself for his poor performance by not eating for the entire day. That night he went to bed very tired and hungry.

He was persistent and kept plugging away, making call after call; and by the end of his first week his production was remarkable. He had sold $92,000 of life insurance. By December he had set a company record for a new six-month agent and had earned $18,000 in commissions. By then, Joe knew what he wanted to do for the rest of his life. He had found a lifetime career!

Carol and their two children joined him in Baton Rouge; for the first time, he saw his daughter. The Gandolfos moved into a new apartment, hired a part-time housekeeper, and for the first time, Joe bought a new car.

Joe credits his initial success to his willingness to work and his strong belief in life insurance. He understood firsthand that bad things happen to a man's wife and children if he dies without providing for them! He was obviously able to communicate this message very well to others. His first year's earnings were $35,000. At his teacher's salary, it would have taken him a dozen years to earn that much!

In 1961, Carol and Joe made the decision to leave Baton Rouge. They had enjoyed Baton Rouge, but they loved Florida's weather. Joe spent two weeks traveling throughout the state in search of his "ideal" community. He picked Lakeland, a town of thirty thousand located in the center of the state. Like Baton Rouge, Lakeland is a college town, the home of Florida Southern.

He had made up his mind to go for his Chartered Life Underwriter designation, and Lakeland had no CLUs. Neither did it have a single life agent who had qualified for the Million Dollar Round Table. He was determined to become the city's first on both scores. As with so many other good fortunes in his life, Joe gives God a lot of the credit. "I prayed hard," he says, "but I worked very hard at the same time."

Lakeland was a good choice. Three years after the Gandolfos' relocation, it was announced that Disney World would be developing in nearby Orlando. Joe was at the right place at the right time. His Disney

World–connected life insurance sales have run into billions.

Some people credit Joe's success to luck, but he was only one of many life insurance agents in Central Florida when Disney World arrived. Some salespersons criticize Joe's work schedule and say that it's been too much of a drain on his family. And there are those who insist that his success is exaggerated. Joe points to a plaque on his wall to express his feelings toward his critics. It reads, *Jealousy is the tribute mediocrity pays to genius.*

While all records are made to be broken, there are some who think that Joe's billion-dollar year will last well into the twenty-first century. Only Joe himself is a candidate to break it; however, much of his time today is spent serving as a tax-shelter consultant to many of his wealthy clients. He is also one of the nation's most sought-after speakers, and has appeared on national television. He's especially proud of his five appearances on the Christian Broadcasting Network—*The 700 Club.* Although his speaking career only generates a fraction of the income he earns from selling life insurance, each year he speaks to at least fifty audiences all over the world.

Joe loves to share the secrets of his success. He thrives on it. For the remainder of this book, Joe will reveal how he sells *billions*—and no matter what you sell, if you do it *the Gandolfo way,* I promise you that your sales production will soar!

HOW TO MAKE BIG MONEY SELLING

1

The Selling Opportunity

For years, Americans had perceived salespeople as fast-talking, joke-telling hustlers who sold by trickery, intimidation, or seduction. Personality was thought to be the most important asset; glibness, a skill to be perfected.

It's been a tough image to shake, though it's understandable. It's rooted in our early history (the medicine men who cried, "I'll tell ya what I'm gonna do"). It's a part of our folk humor ("You hear the one about the traveling salesman and the farmer's daughter?"). It is in our literature, and on our stage and screen (poor Willy Loman in *Death of a Salesman*, Clark Gable's slick-talking adman in *The Hucksters*, and Prof. Harold Hill in *The Music Man*).

The image wasn't helped by the used-car salesmen who preyed on an auto-hungry public after World War II. Nor by the home improvement peddler who arrived on the scene at about the same time and swindled the elderly and the widowed. But these people are *con artists,* not *salespeople.* This book is not for them. I'm writing for the individual who knows that it takes much more to be a professional salesperson than simply the possession of an imposing demeanor, a gift of gab, and a ready victim! I mean those salespeople who strive for excellence in their profession . . . and especially those who have the ambition to be the very best in their field.

Anyone who makes a living by selling for profit is considered a salesperson. This includes the person who interrupts your dinner with a telephone sales pitch, the door-to-door peddler, the clerk in the neighborhood deli, the factory rep, the stockbroker, the literary agent.

The salespeople who fascinate me the most—and with whom I have the greatest empathy—are those entrepreneurial types who take risks and derive their income solely from their selling efforts. In the next pages, I will discuss the various selling arrangements, with special attention to the risks and benefits of each.

The Salesperson's Compensation

The income potential in a selling arrangement between a salesperson and the company is influenced by the following: (1) the personal financial risk the salesperson is willing to take, (2) the financial risk the company is willing to take, (3) the profitability of the product or service being sold, and (4) the percentage of a company's income budgeted for its selling costs.

In general, the greater the risk that you, the salesperson, are willing to take, the greater your opportunity to earn big money. No company in the world, for example, would pay me a guaranteed salary that approaches the money I earn as a free agent taking my own risks. But there are many considerations, many pros and cons to appraise, before you decide exactly which way to go. Let's take a look at the various arrangements under which salespeople are generally compensated:

1. *Straight Salary.* I don't consider an individual who sells on a straight salary to be a professional salesperson. These people are generally salesclerks. They usually work in a retail store and help customers locate items. They may be required to do anything from straightening out stock to dusting fixtures. They get paid for putting in their time—regardless. If they work for a large company, there may be some opportunity eventually to get off the selling floor and become department managers or buyers. They will never make big bucks selling in this environment. However, they will have greater job security, and may receive a benefits package including insurance, paid vacations, annual raises, and participation in a retirement plan. Nevertheless, for even a moderately ambitious salesperson, this is not a good career opportunity.

2. *Salary Plus for the Indoor Salesperson.* The "plus" is often a small bonus or commission that is used as a "carrot" to get the salesclerk to sell slow-moving merchandise or goods with a particularly high profit margin. This type of bonus arrangement will never change a person's standard of living. It's usually small change.

On the other hand, the indoor salesperson is generally covered by company benefits such as social security contributions, health insurance, pension-plan contributions; and paid holidays, vacations, and sick days.

The retailer invests in advertising and location to bring the customer to the salesperson. And it invests in displays and fixtures and incentives to the customer, to help the salesperson write an order. All this costs the company money, so it's understandable that the company is less willing to pay high salaries or commissions to its sales force.

For some people, an indoor sales position offers the maximum security and actually works out best. While it is true that these sales positions are unquestionably among the lowest-paying, some people need a place to go every day and the stability of fixed working hours. I know some people who simply wouldn't do a full day's work if they had the freedom to set their own hours. Lacking the self-discipline to go out and sell every day, they "spin their wheels" and see only a few prospects. I've seen many of these halfhearted salespeople, and they're great at finding excuses for not calling on prospects. They put in what's known as "windowshield time." They spend too much time in between sales presentations, never seeing enough prospects to make a decent living. These salespeople need to work in a controlled environment—and the best place for them may be inside a retail store.

3. *Salary Plus Commission for the Outside Salesperson.* Many outside salespeople work under some sort of arrangement that includes a guaranteed base pay, reimbursement for travel expenses, and an incentive to increase a territory's sales.

The more paternalistic the company, the more stable and predictable the salesperson's paycheck. The most paternalistic company pays a salesperson a "living wage," provides a company car, provides health and life insurance, and offers paid vacations, paid holidays, and sick days—and in addition to all this, has an incentive program that can add up to (but rarely more than) 20 percent of the base pay.

Not a bad job for a lot of people. These companies are often well known and give their salespeople a sense of respectability. Their position is often envied by salespeople who work for competing companies that offer a less generous guaranteed package. And some packages are a lot less generous. However, the more that a company gives you, the more they are apt to take away from you. When somebody pays your salary, they also "buy" certain rights that restrict your freedom. For example, an outside salaried salesman with a company car and an expense account is likely to be accountable for his whereabouts every day. He will have a great deal of paperwork to submit, often on a daily basis. The rationale of management is, "I want to know what I'm getting for the money I'm paying you." Although the salaried salesman may produce a lot of sales, he can anticipate this kind of control on the part of management. After all, the company has every right to tell its employee whom to see and when to make the calls.

Salaried salespeople who are paid bonuses based on production are subject to fluctuating sales quotas; these quota adjustments are used to keep the pay package in line with the company's budgeted commitments. While it can be said that a company should be delighted to pay additional commissions for more business, in the real world it simply doesn't work out that way. In this system, the company may arbitrarily cut territories and reassign important accounts—if by doing so they can reduce costs and increase a territory's profitability. The loser has to be the salesperson. While it may not sound fair, as long as the company is taking all the risks, it is not going to give away more of the profits than is absolutely necessary. Many companies are notorious for employing these tactics, so before you start in a new sales position, you should thoroughly check out these kinds of things.

A good paternalistic company offers more up-front security than most salaried jobs. For me, this type of sales organization is of no interest. I want maximum opportunity, not paternal protection, but I can understand the appeal of this kind of position to many salespeople.

4. *Straight Commission Salesperson with a Draw.* A salesperson who works on a straight commission with a draw is paid solely for what he sells. The company advances him a fixed amount of his anticipated commissions on a regular basis, usually monthly or semimonthly. From the company's point of view, the purpose of the draw is to provide the salesperson with enough money to operate until his commissions are received. The commissions advanced are based on a conservative estimate of what the salesman will produce. If he fails to earn the advance, he is indebted to the company—so the advance is actually a loan. Some companies will require a salesperson to sign an agreement which states that unearned advances must be paid back. Other companies, knowing that it may be difficult to collect commissions advanced, do not require a written agreement, but they are careful to monitor sales volume, making sure the salesperson does not fall deeply in debt. If a salesman fails to pro-

duce at a certain level, his draw may be reduced or terminated (and so might his job).

In some industries, draws are necessary because there is a long period before a new salesperson actually produces. A new insurance agent can go weeks or months before making enough sales to support a family; he might not be able to survive without this sort of financial aid.

In other cases, a draw is necessary even for established salespeople, especially in industries where a long period elapses between the time an order is taken and the time the commission is paid. For instance, a manufacturer's representative might sell a retail store a large order in September for goods to be shipped in March and paid for in May. Commissions aren't due until the goods are paid for, so any payment to the salesperson prior to May is actually an advance. If, for any reason, the manufacturer is not paid, the advance is charged back to the salesperson. Remember, the advance is only a loan.

A salesperson whose income is derived primarily from commissions may be able to negotiate some fringe benefits (insurance, perhaps) from the company he represents, but he will never receive benefits as great as a salaried employee.

5. *The Straight Commission Salesperson.* The opposite of the salaried salesperson is the straight commission independent rep. He is an independent contractor—he pays 100 percent of all his expenses and receives no fringe benefits. He pays Social Security as a self-employed person; and when he doesn't work on holidays or vacations, he doesn't make money. Likewise, he doesn't get paid on days when he is sick!

At first, it appears that the totally independent straight commission salesman has a bad deal. He must pay for all of his overhead, and it's possible that, at times, his expenses will exceed his earnings. And even when his business is doing well, he might have to wait several months until he gets paid. In my business, I don't receive a commission on a life insurance policy until the issuance date and the collected premium are submitted to the company. If an applicant's medical information is delayed, it could be several months before my commission is paid.

The straight commission sales position presents some serious drawbacks, but it also offers some important advantages. First, it gives you the most independence—and I treasure my freedom. I don't have to report to anyone—I am my own boss! Second, the commissions schedules are somewhat higher than those used by companies that provide fringe benefits. In theory, if a straight commission salesperson does exceptionally well, the higher commission rates will more than pay for benefits he would have otherwise received. I am much better off working on this basis, and so is every big producer. My philosophy is: Pay me at the highest possible rate of commissions and let me take care of myself. Don't give me a car. I'll buy my own. And let me pay for my own insurance—and everything else. Just don't put a ceiling on my earnings, and I'll decide how to spend my money. While the top salespeople always benefit from this arrangement, the lowest producers usually suffer. They would do better with lower commission rates and the company's covering expenses. For salespeople of middling performance, it's a toss-up. Keep in mind, however, that after some time, if it becomes unprofitable for the company, the low-producing salesman will get his walking papers!

Our free-enterprise system dictates that those of us who take the most business risks are most likely to receive the highest returns for our efforts; and straight commission selling does indeed comply with this dictum. But, I caution you: risk-taking is not for everyone! A novice salesperson, for instance, may need the security of a salary or draw instead of being paid straight commissions. He may not have the accumulated savings needed to cover his business and personal expenses until he achieves a steady, predictable income. Burdened with a high personal overhead, he may not be able to survive the long wait for commission checks. For some, working on a straight commission creates too much stress. It's definitely not recommended for the fainthearted! So, while the more secure, guaranteed basis for compensation may not offer the maximum potential, it clearly fulfills the needs of many salespeople.

Is the Sky the Limit?

"The sky is the limit in selling," does not apply to the majority of salespeople, as I've pointed out above. The more dependent one is on his company for security, the lower the earning potential. One salesperson put it this way: "I get nervous when my company offers me something for nothing. They never gave me anything that they didn't take away from me first."

Many direct-selling, multilevel companies solicit people with the pitch, "The sky is the limit"; and for a few individuals, they do indeed deliver. However, the big money is not earned by one's ability to sell a product but by one's strong recruiting and training efforts. Most direct-sales products are small-ticket items (soap, brushes, cosmetics), and of course earn small commissions per sale. There aren't enough hours in the day to make big money—even if you sold to every prospect. Only by "leveraging" your efforts (having *many* people selling for you) can you earn a lot of money. One multilevel organization claims to have more than one million independent sales agents, and they boast a billion-dollar sales volume! It doesn't take a mathematical genius to figure out that their average salesperson is generating annual sales of approximately one thousand dollars! With a commission in the neighborhood of 25 percent, the typical salesperson is earning $250 a year! When you consider that some of its top distributors are earning several hundred thousand dollars annually, the average salesperson is making less than five dollars a week!

"So who wants to be average?" these companies ask. "If *you* work hard, the sky is the limit," they tell you. Maybe so, but you'd better go into this business with your eyes wide open. In the multilevel sales industry, you can't get rich from selling a product. Your real job will be to recruit, train, and motivate others to sell for you. It's not the same game as straight commission selling.

It's the big-ticket items such as multimillion-dollar insurance policies, securities, and commercial real estate that offer the most potential through individual selling efforts. And while these fields are not too difficult to break into, they do require a salesperson to "earn his spurs" before he makes really big money. By earning one's spurs, I mean becoming well established as an expert in the field. In this type of sales position, you must build a reputation before you can sell in large quantities and establish a clientele with enough money to buy your product. Such reputations are built on your willingness and ability to serve your clients. Over a period of time, the majority of your sales will result from repeat business and referrals. I will talk more about this subject in a later chapter.

The truly big money in sales comes from the straight commission high-risk positions; and in effect, at this level you actually run your own business. In my case, for example, I have my own office building, six full-time, well-paid secretaries, a full-time accountant, a WATS line, and a very sophisticated computer. I also travel approximately 100,000 miles every year, and I pay for every dime of it. In short, I have my work cut out for me—but I am also very well compensated for my efforts. My business generates enough in sales to pay for all of my overhead, and at the end of the year there's a healthy profit. But as I said, there *is* a risk, and it's not for everyone.

What's the Right Product for You?

You should give as much thought to choosing a product or service to sell as you do to choosing the type of sales career to pursue.

What your financial goals are, of course, will have an impact on your choice. If you want to get rich, don't select a product with a low price, a narrow profit margin, and a slow turnover rate.

There are other considerations, not directly related to profit and income. I strongly recommend that you sell something that really excites you. For one thing, it's a joy to honestly project conviction and enthusiasm for your product and it's contagious. I am lucky enough to be so high about my product that I can't wait to go to work each day. Consequently, I work long hours and have fun doing so.

It simply makes sense to sell a product that interests you. For example, a person with musical talent might be happiest selling musical instruments; a weekend artist might excel in selling art supplies; a handyman could be especially skillful selling "how-to" equipment; a person who loves beautiful things might enjoy selling to elegant boutiques. I could fill this book with these kinds of connections, but you get the idea.

The product you choose to sell will determine your work environment to a great extent. And that can be an important consideration. Do you want to spend your time on construction sites or on farms? In bakeries or factories? In bookstores or grocery stores? Do you want to spend your time selling in busy shopping centers or in private homes?

The product you choose will also determine the type of people you will deal with and the level of tension to which you will be subjected.

All of these factors will affect the quality of your workday. If you can, choose a selling position that will turn you on—one that will bring you joy in addition to money. You deserve the best situation that you can possibly design for yourself.

I'm not saying that you must have the perfect product in order to be financially successful, although I know of some cases that seem to contradict that.

I know a super real-estate agent who originally failed as a life insurance agent. I know a man who was a down-and-out car salesman and is now the leading stockbroker in his community. I don't know how many would-be salespeople quit selling because they don't succeed with a particular product, but I do know that it's great to sell a product you really believe in to a prospect you can identify with in an environment that nurtures you!

Again, from a financial point of view, there's a wide range of methods by which a salesperson is compensated. Just what's best for you requires a lot of investigation and thought.

Your decision for selecting the sales position with the best opportunity shouldn't only be influenced by monetary considerations. You must also ask yourself what will provide you with enjoyment and maximum job satisfaction. Choosing the right career is somewhat like choosing the right spouse. You should be looking for a long and happy relationship.

Just as you must be the one to decide what's best for you, I personally chose to maintain the maximum independence; and accordingly, I take the maximum risks. I sell big-ticket items on straight commission because they generate large commissions per sale. Going this route has worked very well for me, and throughout this book I will share my selling philosophies and techniques with you. I hope that they work well for you too.

2

The Making of a Great
Salesperson

It makes no sense to me when people say that so-and-so is a "natural-born" salesperson. After all, is there such a thing as a natural-born doctor, attorney, or dentist?

The natural-born salesperson is supposed to have an outgoing personality—be an attractive extrovert with eloquent expressive powers—a smooth manipulative charmer. Psychologists have helped to ingrain this notion. A typical question on an aptitude test for applicants for a sales position reads: "List the following in the order of your preference: (a) A quiet evening reading a book, (b) A large, elegant party with many strangers, (c) A small, intimate party with a few close friends, or (d) Dinner with a single close friend."

If you have to take such an aptitude test, I recommend you answer the above questions as follows: b, c, d, and a. The stereotyped salesperson is supposed to love being around large crowds. "Introverts should steer clear of a career in sales! They haven't got a chance," say the proponents of the natural-born salesperson theory.

If they are right, I certainly don't belong in sales. To start with, I don't have an outgoing personality. I speak very softly and fast, and sometimes my Southern Kentucky accent makes me sound as if I'm mumbling. I am a loner. The order of my answer to the above multiple-choice question would be: a, d, c, and b. I'd like to meet the psychologists who design these tests. It's a good bet that they never sold anything.

When I attended my first Million Dollar Round Table conventions, I studied the top-producing agents to see what was so unusual about them—perhaps they shared some unusual traits. But they didn't seem any different from any other group of professional people. They could have been dentists, attorneys, or engineers.

I've had an opportunity to meet many of the top salespeople in the country, and it's only coincidence when a super salesperson fits the stereotyped description. I'm not suggesting that a golden-throat speaking voice isn't a good trait for a salesperson. It just isn't necessary, that's all. So if you've got one, that's wonderful; I'm not knocking it. And if you have complete control of the language, that's good too. But, I've met too many top salespeople who stutter, mumble, and speak broken English to know that you don't have to sound like Jane Pauley or Dan Rather to make it big in the sales field.

Several years ago, I heard one of the nation's leading insurance agents give a speech at a convention, and he spoke behind a curtain! He was too shy to face the large audience. His voice was gravelly and he had a thick foreign accent—but everyone listened intently because he was a super salesman and they knew it.

A Winning Attitude

Two of my idols are the late great football coach Vince Lombardi of the Green Bay Packers and George Allen, the former coach of the Washington Redskins and Los Angeles Rams. I frequently quote them in my speeches, especially when I talk about a winning attitude and discipline. We know that natural ability will only take an athlete so far. In order to win, he must have tremendous discipline. And to Lombardi and Allen, winning was everything. At the end of a sports event, success is easily measured.

I like to draw comparisons between sports and selling because, in both, success can be measured easily. You know exactly how well you did. You either score, or you don't. You either experience the joy of winning or the agony of defeat.

I love sports the way I love selling. It's the competition that turns me on. Lombardi once said:

It's a reality of life that men are competitive, and the most competitive games draw the most competitive men. That's why they are there, to compete and to win. They know the rules and the objectives when they get in the game. The objective is to win—fairly, squarely, decently, by the rules—but to win.

Football is a heck of a game—so is selling.

People at seminars say to me, "Joe, you've made millions. Do you still get upset when you don't make a sale?" Of course it bothers me, because I hate to lose. It's not the money that motivates me—I haven't been motivated by money for years. I'm motivated by the challenge and the sense of accomplishment I get from doing a good job. I strive to be number one. As John F. Kennedy put it, "Once you say you're going to settle for second, that's what happens to you in life, I find."

So it still bothers me to lose a sale. I want to sell every person I call on. Show me a salesperson who doesn't *mind* losing, and I'll *show* you a loser. I'm in the business to win.

The Importance of Discipline

A professional salesperson's success requires the same intense discipline that is found in sports. My first three months as a salesman were spent away from my family, putting in hundred-hour work weeks in Baton Rouge. I figured that three months of backbreaking effort was a small price to pay to give my new vocation a fair chance. I had barely enough money to pay my $35 monthly rent; I had nowhere to go, and nothing to do *except work.* There were no distractions, nothing to come home to every night.

Admittedly, there were nights when I felt unbearably homesick for my wife and small son. The worst times were when I spent eighteen hours in the field and came back to that small, lonely room without a sale to show for my long day. I locked myself in the room, got down on my knees, and asked God for guidance. Was I doing the right thing? Was I sacrificing too much? Was I asking too much of my family? Somehow I got the strength and reassurance from prayer.

Each morning I was up by five, attended Mass by six, and made calls for the rest of the day until ten at night. I only ate one meal a day—after work—and if I had had a bad day, I skipped that meal. For the next ten years of my life, I followed the same routine—one meal a day, after work. And I continued to fast when there were no sales. This is what I did. I'm not suggesting it for you.

An industrial psychologist who gave me a series of tests commented, "You've got the highest threshold of pain of any person I ever tested." I told him that I just don't let anything stop me from accomplishing what I'm after.

I wanted to succeed so badly I could taste it. My faith in God and hard work consumed every moment of my life. I remembered a quote from Augustine that helped me: "Pray as though everything depended on God. Work as though everything depended on you." I *knew* God would guide me, but it was *I* who must work. If I didn't succeed, it wouldn't be due to a lack of hard work!

To anyone striving to make it big, I recommend that you go out there and *work* six full days a week—and I'm talking about getting up at five or six and working until ten each night until you can smell success. If you're willing to pay that kind of price, you'll develop good work habits that will last a lifetime. And you'll be miles ahead of your average competitor.

One of my favorite stories is about the swallows that arrive at Capistrano, California, every March 19, not one day early nor one day late—after a six-thousand-mile trip across the ocean from Argentina. And then every October—they make the return trip. Now, those little birds can't swim, nor can they fly that long distance nonstop—but for years, nobody knew how they made their amazing biannual journey.

Then it was observed that the swallows would pick up a twig each time they left to cross the ocean. Now, a twig is a big burden for a little swallow to take on such a long trip. But it is carried because, when the swallow gets tired, he puts the twig down onto the water to float. Then he stands on it and rests. After resting for a while, he picks up the twig and flies off again.

I like this story because it illustrates how the swallow is willing to pay the price of carrying a burden in order to reach his destination. There was no shortcut. No magic. There never has been; there never will be. Not for the swallows and not for any of us.

> Nothing will take the place of persistence; talent will not; nothing is more common than unsuccessful men with talent. Genius will not; unrewarded genius is almost a proverb. Education will not; the world is full of educated derelicts. Persistence and determination are omnipotent.

Calvin Coolidge said that—but not nearly so often as I have.

Use of Time

"Time is money." You've heard that a thousand times, but it's more than a cliché when we're talking about a salesperson. Unlike a salaried, nine-to-five employee, a salesman's time is his own. As an independent contractor, he has the flexibility to work his own pace and his own hours. His success is, by and large, dependent upon how wisely his time is used. There are 1,440 minutes in a day, and the more you cherish each of those precious minutes, the more productive you will be. As Lord Chesterfield said, "I recommend you take care of the minutes, for the hours will take care of themselves." And I'll add to his quote that the hours take care of the days, weeks, and months.

I get up two hours earlier than most salespeople who get up at seven, so I increase my six-day work week by twelve hours. At the same time, if I add on an extra two hours at the end of each day, I'm putting in an extra twenty-four hours each week. Based on the typical eight-hour day, I'm putting in an extra three days a week; or during a fifty-week year, an extra 150 days! Now, there's no way that I'm not going to be more productive than the person who won't work like that!

In addition to working a long day, a secret is to get the most mileage out of your time. During my working hours, I don't do a single activity that has no purpose. Every meal has a purpose. If I eat with somebody, he's either a client or somebody who can help me to make money. If I eat alone, I'm either on the phone or reading something that has to do with my business. Every person I speak to during the day is work-related. Everything I read is directly or indirectly associated with my business.

I think people put too much time into eating and sleeping. My greatest wish is that there would be some way that I didn't have to sleep or eat! To me, any meal that lasts more than fifteen to twenty minutes is unproductive time—and for the most part, a bad habit.

I also believe that a salesperson should eat his

breakfast only with a potential customer. For the first ten years in my career, I never ate breakfast or lunch unless it was to give a sales presentation. Sure, those meals cost money; but when you consider the small investment of a few dollars in comparison to the return from making a sale, picking up the tab is a real bargain. This is one area where some salespeople penny-pinch—which, I believe, is foolish. Many of my finest sales have been made during these meals with people whom I might otherwise have never met. Many clients who had initially refused to give me an interview gave in when I said, "Look, you have to eat! When do you eat lunch? How about breakfast?"

I'd end up getting an appointment, and there were many, many days when I'd meet with one prospect for breakfast at six and have just a glass of orange juice with him. Then at seven, I'd rush off to have breakfast with somebody else and eat perhaps just a piece of toast. Then I'd have a cup of coffee with somebody else during a breakfast meeting at eight.

Not too long ago, a young man came to me and asked for my advice on how he could double his sales production, which at the time was $2.5 million. I asked him to tell me about his typical day, and he said, "I get up at about seven each morning, have breakfast with my wife and kids, then I take the kids to school and get to the office just before nine."

"That's all I have to hear," I replied. "Stop right there."

"I don't understand," he said.

"You're wasting half your life," I told him. "You don't sell your wife and kids at breakfast, and you don't get paid for taking them to school. Now, if that's what you want to do, then fine. But don't come to me and say you want to double your production. It takes sacrifice; and in this case, unfortunately, it's sacrificing some time with your family."

After we talked awhile and he realized just how much it was costing him to have breakfast with his wife and kids, he thought about it and said, "You know something, Joe, I don't even talk to them in the morning. At the breakfast table I read the newspaper and the kids watch TV. Then, while I'm driving them to school, my mind is so much on my work, there's very little conversation in the car." He stood up, shook my hand, and thanked me for advice he insisted would help him realize his ambition. He was smart enough to follow it, and sure enough, the following year his production had nearly tripled!

Over the years, I have observed that successful people are the ones who get up early to go to work. And because they do, they respect a salesperson who's willing to do the same thing. When an insurance agent asks to see a businessman during his workday and gets turned down, the prospect is saying, "You work nine to five, and those are also my working hours. I make my money then, and I don't want to take that time to help you make money."

I get around this kind of thinking by saying, "Can I see you at six-thirty on Tuesday morning, or would seven-thirty be better?" When he hears me say this, he translates it to my saying, "Let's talk when you're not busy making money. Let's talk when you can concentrate on what I'm saying. I'm on call twenty-four hours a day to serve you. When are you not making money? We can talk then." I can promise you that for most successful people, that time will be between 6:30 and 8:30 in the morning. Or it will be at noon or between 5:00 and 8:00 P.M. The majority of my sales have been before nine in the morning.

The person who gets up early thinks, "I want to do business with somebody who also gets up early." He thinks, "This guy works as hard at his job as I do at mine." I believe that self-made people get to where they are by working very hard, and I have found that hardworking people don't like loafers.

In my third year in the insurance business, I sold my first $1 million policy. An attorney who saw me at six o'clock Mass every morning left his card under my windshield with a message to call on him. He was impressed that I was such an early riser, he said. He introduced me to an elderly woman who he thought needed more insurance. That introduction resulted in my first $1 million sale!

It's paramount for every salesperson to realize that nothing should interfere with his selling time. The most important use of your time is being eyeball-to-eyeball with clients. During my first ten years in the business, my total efforts were in giving sales presentations scheduled every ninety minutes—beginning as early in the morning as I could see somebody and continuing until ten each night. I always had backup prospects to call on, so if an appointment busted, I'd have somebody else to see. These backups were existing clients who lived in the area, or perhaps somebody who had canceled an appointment previously. I'd walk in cold with those people, hoping to get something going to fill in the time before my next call. Cold calls are not the best calls, but they're better than seeing no one. These were the only circumstances when I'd ever make them. One of the things that I have always enjoyed about selling is that it always keeps me busy because there's always something to do. I try my darnedest to fill in all the gaps so my time will be well spent.

While eyeball-to-eyeball selling is the best use of a salesperson's time, prospecting is firmly in second place. Whenever there was any extra time between calls, there were all kinds of things I'd do to find new prospects. I'd call existing clients for referrals, look for new business announcements in the newspaper, and scan new business ads in the yellow pages. My eyes were always open for leads. This "down time" was also used to set up future appointments, and I'd arrange them up to two and three weeks in advance. Occasionally, broken-appointment time was used to deliver policies.

It was very important to keep myself busy when there was a lull in my schedule. I felt that appearing to be busy was also good for my image. I think it's extremely poor judgment for a professional salesperson to stop in a local restaurant and be seen drinking coffee, killing time. For obvious reasons, a cocktail lounge would be even worse! I would go to extremes to avoid appearing as if I had nothing to do. If necessary, I'd even go to the local library and get some business-oriented reading done, something I'd have to read sooner or later anyhow.

Incidentally, when I'd schedule my daily appointments, I'd always arrange them logistically to avoid wasting a lot of time in my car. I saved on gas money, and maximized my prime selling time. Even today, when I travel across the country calling on my multimillionaire clients, I arrange them according to location. When I go to the West Coast to call on my clients, I spend several days out there calling on many of them. The planning is the same wherever I go.

Today I work at a slower pace than my first ten years in the business. I've paid my dues, so I don't have to work the same backbreaking schedule (although, compared to other salespeople, I still outwork them). Nowadays I set up appointments for estate planning and tax-sheltering, and I'm booked up twelve months in advance. I charge a consulting fee of $1,000 to people who come to Lakeland at their own expense. The fee is fixed regardless of the length of the consultation. In addition to helping them with their estate planning, I sell them tax-shelter investments and large life insurance policies. My consultations start at 8:30 each morning and continue until about noon. During the early afternoon, I head for the tennis court and put in a good two hours every day. Then I come back to the office and take between thirty and forty telephone calls a day. After office hours, I'll read or work with my computer until bedtime—between nine and ten each night.

As I mentioned early on, I delegate everything that other people can do for me. It's a matter of simple arithmetic. If I can pay them less than what my time's worth, I let them do it—particularly the things where they're as effective as I am. I avoid all busywork. Too many people waste their time going to the bank, writing checks, and picking up the mail. My tailor comes to my office, and so does my barber. I even have a sauna, workout room, and sun deck at my office. There's also a kitchen so time isn't wasted having to go out to eat.

In fact, my entire staff eats at the office so nobody wastes time.

During the past several years, I have been actively involved in consulting large associations such as automobile dealer associations and savings-and-loan associations. A lot of my time has also been devoted to speeches which I have delivered in every state in the union, Canada, Central and South America, and throughout Europe. This time has paid off handsomely because, in addition to generating high speaker's fees, members of the audience will later call or write to ask for a consultation. These requests keep two full-time employees busy handling the calls and setting up appointments. Consequently, with my staff servicing existing accounts and handling new insurance needs— along with the call-ins and write-ins—my annual sales production has maintained a very high level although I'm not now working a sixteen-hour day. As I said, I've paid my dues.

What does good time-management really boil down to? In a nutshell, it's a matter of discipline and priorities. You must decide what you want. You can't have everything, and life is full of compromises. You've got to sacrifice something. If you want to be an outstanding golfer more than you want to be a great salesperson, that's fine, but don't expect to become a scratch golfer and maintain high sales production too. Again I say: There's a price you must pay for everything.

The Theory of Ratios

Selling is a numbers game. When I first began in the business, I was quickly indoctrinated. My sales manager instilled the idea that if I made two hundred calls each week, I'd get fifteen appointments, resulting in one sale. That didn't sound too swift, but I believed in the numbers. I figured I'd increase the numbers and increase the bottom line—getting more sales.

I was aware that I lacked finesse, so I had to rely on seeing large numbers of people. I knew that if I made enough calls, I'd get not only more than my share of sales, but I'd also increase my selling skills. Eventually I'd get more appointments per number of calls and more sales per number of appointments. All the numbers would fall right into place. I knew that the theory of ratios always works. If you flip a coin enough times in the air, it will average 50 percent heads and 50 percent tails. But with only a few tosses, say ten, the numbers don't work. And if you flip heads five times in a row, the odds are still 50-50 that the next toss will be tails.

Did you know that when Babe Ruth was the home-run king, he also struck out more than anyone else? Selling works on the same principle. In the beginning, you get a lot of noes in order to get the yesses. But if you hang in there long enough, you'll get them. Persistence is vital in making the theory of ratios work. Benjamin Disraeli said, "The secret of success is constancy to purpose."

Physical Fitness

Your physical fitness has a lot to do with your sales career. First and foremost, being physically fit is a matter of discipline, and discipline is a quality that you can't turn on when you go to work each morning. If you are a disciplined person, you apply it on and off the job. You can't be one person during your working hours and another during your nonworking hours.

For better or worse, you are judged by your appearance. Remember that you only get one chance to make a first impression. When an overstuffed person walks into a prospect's office, the first impression is, "If he doesn't take care of his body, he must have low self-esteem." The prospect may also conclude that if you lack discipline in your personal life, you also will lack it in business and therefore not be reliable nor give him good service.

Keeping physically fit gives you the stamina to work long hours. If you don't take good care of yourself, you'll end up dragging yourself to your late-afternoon and early-evening appointments lacking the pep and enthusiasm it takes to give an effective sales presentation.

Don't ever go into a sales interview on a full stomach. You're apt to be sluggish. And too much sugar in your system might make you too volatile. The salesperson who takes care of his body has a sharper brain. Your health is bound to affect how you react. Out-of-shape salespeople aren't as attentive; they simply won't hear everything that's being said. When you're run down physically, you simply can't function efficiently, and when it comes to working . . . forget it.

I strongly recommend that you participate in a physical-fitness program that includes a healthful diet and daily exercise. I won't suggest any particular programs; I'll leave the choice up to you. I follow a strict macrobiotic diet, mostly vegetables, grains, rice, and seaweed. I believe that most health problems result from overeating, and Americans are guilty of spending too much time at the dinner table. As Benjamin Franklin put it, "To lengthen thy life, lessen thy meals."

For those of you who say you can't find the time to exercise, I say nonsense. I believe that an hour of exercise is more valuable than an hour of sleep. If you can't find the time, knock off an hour of sleep each night. You're probably getting more sleep than you need anyhow.

The Spouse's Role

My wife, Carol, has played a major role in my success. Without her support, I doubt if I could have made it—it's that simple.

When I first started my sales career, I told Carol, "Look, I am going to work eighteen hours a day, seven days a week for an entire year. Time will be our big initial investment in this career." It was a tremendous sacrifice for Carol, too, because we had so little time together. There's no question that my long hours cut into our social life. And it meant Carol would have to attend PTA meetings, Little League games, and piano recitals without me.

She also knew that my work required 100 percent of my concentration; that I couldn't cope with many of the problems that, ordinarily, we would have dealt with together or that I might have had to work out myself. She took over the complete management of our household.

There was no reason for me to know about appliances that went on the blink. She called up the repairmen and had things fixed. I never received a call in the middle of the day like other husbands: "Joe, what am I going to do? There's no air-conditioning in the house!" She became a terrific manager and I was able to devote my full energies to what I do best—and that's selling life insurance. I didn't have to worry about the kinds of problems I wasn't any good at in the first place and she didn't have to worry about my screwing things up at home.

Of course I realize that, today, many women also have careers, and many of them are in sales. With this in mind, I know that in the two-career family it's not always possible to have one spouse take care of things as Carol does. As more than one professional woman has said to me, "What I need is a wife!"

But what does the two-career family do? First, a couple can work out an equitable way to delegate responsibilities so neither one becomes overburdened. Second, a couple should hire help to do the chores neither one likes nor has the time to do. For example, unless you enjoy cutting the grass, you're better off paying a high-school kid to do it and spending the extra time selling. Over a period of time, you'll surely be many dollars ahead. The same thing applies to shoveling snow, cleaning windows, doing laundry, and doing general repairs around the house. My philosophy has always been that people with high earning capacities should never do the things they don't enjoy if those same hours can be spent in the field instead.

Every so often when I speak about working long, hard hours, people say to me, "Hey, Joe, all that work isn't good for a marriage." Maybe not, but look at the people who are getting divorced; for the most part, they're the ones who work nine to five. They spend too much time with each other—*that's* their problem! There's too much emphasis put on togetherness, and husbands and wives feel guilty about not being with each other. But you should never feel guilty about working. It's the quality, not the quantity, of time you spend with your family. Every Saturday night I'd date my wife, and Sunday has always been family day for us. You see, God worked six days and rested one. It was man who invented long weekends, vacations, and retirement; and as far as I'm concerned, I don't want them.

So, the making of a super successful salesperson is a matter of putting the whole act together. It takes a healthy body, a winning attitude and incredible self-discipline, and a good support system at home. Also, if you're going to apply the theory of ratios, you must be willing to work long, hard hours, sacrificing most of your leisure time. You must treat your working time as though it were a precious commodity. *Do not waste it!*

3

What to Do *Before* the Sale

If you have ambitions to excel as a highly paid professional salesperson, you *must* make it your business to become an expert in your field. You *must* be well-informed and properly prepared before each presentation is scheduled. The professional salesperson has as great a responsibility to his client as any other professional person. A surgeon who enters the operating room without being properly prepared is setting himself up for a malpractice suit. The unprepared fighter who dares to enter the ring against a formidable opponent is risking his very life. An actor who steps on stage without knowing his lines is inviting the wrath of his audience and critics. And a salesperson who walks into a prospect's office without knowing his stuff is just as certain to fail as any other unprepared professional.

Doing Your Homework

John W. Galbreath, one of America's premier real-estate developers, has a lot to say about the importance of doing one's homework: "You've got to know *everything* about your business. There's nothing more disrespectful or presumptuous than going into a man's office and not being able to make it worth his time, not being able to answer his questions, not being able to justify why you're there. If he asks a question related to your business and you reply, 'I don't know,' then you wasted his time. You owe that person an apology because either you're not very good at your own business—not well enough prepared—or you've failed to consider the other person. In either case, you've made a fool of yourself and insulted him."

Every salesperson should know his business backward and forward. You must become an expert in your field if you want to attain maximum success. The best place to start is with your company's training program. You must assume that the company wants you to succeed. Do exactly what they tell you, and if you fail, it will be their fault, not yours.

Don't be one of those people who starts out by ignoring your company's expertise. *Do it the proven way. Don't buck the system. Master it!* And only after your production has soared should you consider making improvements in your presentation. Even then, you should make your changes very cautiously. Don't make them just for the sake of changing things. And don't argue with success. As they say back in my home state of Kentucky, "If it works, don't fix it."

I've seen companies give a new salesperson a fine and proven sales presentation, but it doesn't work because he doesn't execute it properly. Another salesperson goes out there with the same ammunition and he does a bang-up job. Why? It's the difference between a good and a bad actor playing the same role. So, knowing how to say it can be as important as knowing what to say.

How well should a salesman know his product? If you've ever been in the U.S. Army, you well remember how you were required to take your M-1 rifle apart and reassemble it until you could do it blindfolded. The military had good reason for making sure you could reassemble your own weapon. Your life would depend on that ability if your rifle jammed in combat. Similarly, you should know your product inside and out—because your livelihood depends on it.

A word of caution, however: While you must be totally prepared, it isn't always necessary to tell everything you know about your product. Too many technical details can confuse a prospect, so don't tell him everything just to show how smart you are. I do recommend that you know the basics so you can handle general questions that prospects are likely to ask. An automobile salesman should prepare himself by asking his mechanics for explanations about the questions he's most frequently asked. Likewise, a computer salesperson should sit down with his technical people and grill them for the information he needs.

Every salesperson should become self-educated. You should get in the habit of reading everything you can get that pertains to your business. I make an effort to read every important book that's released pertaining to life insurance, estate planning, and taxation. And I read every journal published in my field.

Every salesperson must put aside several hours each week to keep current with what's happening in his field. A life insurance agent must be familiar with the latest information on estate planning and taxation so he can properly advise his clients. A real-estate agent must be in tune with his marketplace and with all of the factors that affect it. A stockbroker must read and know what's happening on Wall Street every day. And in the ever-changing computer industry, the salesperson who isn't a reader will quickly become out of date. *Anyone* who doesn't keep up with the times soon becomes outdated!

I recommend that every salesperson regularly attend seminars and sales meetings. This is an excellent source of information and a good place to meet successful people in your field. Associating with sales leaders and picking their brains is an inexpensive way to pick up knowledge that won't be found in the textbooks. And don't be shy about asking your competition for advice at association seminars. You'll be surprised how willing friendly competitors are about sharing selling tips—if you ask them for their advice. Successful people are generally flattered to be asked such questions as: "Tell me how you have become so successful." "I'm just new in the business. What was it like for you when you were first in the business? Have things changed a great deal since then?" "You're an expert in this business; what do you think will sell next season?" When they tell you, *listen.*

Another source of good information is to read all available information about your competition (their brochures, articles in trade journals, sales literature). I recommend that you go as far as "shopping" for their products or services. "What's so good about your product?" you might ask a salesman, and listen carefully to what he stresses as his strong selling points. "How is it better than XYZ's (your company's) product?'' you might also inquire. Observe how he might knock your company and product. A BMW salesperson, for example, might spend an off hour or two visiting a Mercedes showroom, listening to a complete presentation and taking home brochures. What better way to learn how the competition sells than straight from the horse's mouth—from one of their own salespeople!

Learning as much as possible about your competition is essential because, if you don't, you'll be in the dark when an indecisive customer says, "I want to shop around before I make a decision." If you've done your homework properly, you can say, "Why spend your time shopping around? I'm an expert. You can ask me anything you want to know and I'll tell you." When you really are an expert, he will know it and he will become *your* customer.

Use Prime Selling Time Effectively

Becoming an expert in your field is vital, but never spend your prime selling time at home reading how to become one! Do your homework when it's not possible to be in the field selling. I get up at five o'clock each morning, and before going to church, I read for an hour. It's an ideal time for me—quiet and without interruptions. I also read before I go to bed in the evenings and, when I can, on weekends. I take care of all my non-selling-related business when it is impossible to be in the field. The point is, if you are going to be a top salesperson, you *must* give top priority to face-to-face selling. Yet, it's very important that you make time for study and self-improvement.

You can learn a lot by listening to cassettes while

driving your car, jogging, and even while showering. I get a charge out of watching busy people in Manhattan who walk and jog in traffic with their cassette players and earplugs. You'll also see the same people making use of their time by reading in the subways and taxicabs. Cassette players are a terrific learning aid because they make it possible for us to accomplish two things at once. I simply won't buy the excuse that a salesperson doesn't have enough time to become an expert. There's plenty of time for everyone.

Delegate Part of the Load

My time is worth a lot of money, so anything that I do is expensive. I'm high-priced labor, so anytime that I can delegate a job, I'm saving money.

Let me tell you how I run my office today, but keep in mind that I didn't start off this way. I have seven people on my payroll. My comptroller has been with me for twenty-one years, and calculates the financial details used in my sales presentations; he handles all of the accounting and bookkeeping in my office, and is responsible for customer service. My assistants handle my speaking engagements and travel arrangements, customer complaints, and help in the preparation of my speeches; they also handle the mailing of my brochures, tape cassettes, and books. Two assistants are constantly on the telephone following up leads and prospecting for me.

Everyone in the office is 100-percent sales-oriented, and the customer always comes first. My people have been trained to think as I do. The *number one* concern in our office is: "Is it right for the customer?"

Everybody in my office has an insurance license, and they all service my existing clients. I have an arrangement with them so they can receive commissions for this work in addition to their salaries. Believe me, they are very well paid. My policy has also been to pay top dollar for the very best people, and today I have the highest-paid staff in town. I'm fortunate to have developed a staff of dedicated people whose philosophies and values are compatible with my own.

People say I'm a stickler for details, and I suppose they have a good point. I ask every job applicant if he will allow me to inspect his car. If the interior of the car is messy, I won't hire the person. If he isn't neat in his personal life, the same sloppy habits are likely to carry over to the office. I am a perfectionist who agrees with Winston Churchill's statement, "It is not enough to do your best; sometimes it is necessary to do what is required."

Every salesperson must realize that the most valuable use of his time is giving sales presentations. Nothing that I can possibly do is so productive as the time I spend eyeball-to-eyeball with clients. With this in mind, any other use of my time is insignificant. Too many salespeople fail to realize this, and they waste time running errands such as going to the bank. *You must learn to delegate this work; have somebody else do the non-sales-related work for you.* Save wear and tear on yourself by placing a high value on your time. You'll never be a star salesperson until you do.

Sure, I know what some readers may be thinking: "That's fine for Gandolfo. He can afford to hire others to do his legwork, but I'm not making enough money to hire anyone." Chances are, you can't afford *not* to engage help. Now, I don't expect you to go out and burden yourself with an overhead that your present sales volume doesn't warrant. I'm not suggesting that you set up an organization like mine—the expenses would wipe you out before you even got started! But certainly your time is worth more than the cost of a high-school student to do your errands, typing, and other miscellaneous chores. In fact, in most communities it's possible to find students who will work for the experience, for very little pay, and sometimes for nothing! So, don't fall into a trap that wastes or erodes your valuable selling time. And if your time isn't more valuable than a high-school student's, you'd better start looking for other employment.

Be a Goal-Oriented Person

It's been said that nobody ever gets anywhere without a road map. A salesperson's road map consists of his short-term and long-term plans and goals—because, without them, he will wander aimlessly. For ten years, I set daily and weekly sales goals for myself. Those made it possible for me to achieve my long-term goals. What I reached for was a specific number of sales each week. This worked better for me than dollar goals. I knew that if I could produce the number of sales that I projected, the dollars would be there. I don't think that it matters much what system of planning you use, but it's imperative that you set goals and have a plan to reach them. Definite sales objectives give you direction and help you to monitor your progress. It's a way of keeping score. For me, it adds a certain excitement. I'm a competitor, and I like competing with myself.

I never kept my goals a secret. Once they were put down on paper and known to others, my pride drove me to achieve them. It would have been downright embarrassing to admit that I had fallen short. I think too many people keep their goals to themselves because they're afraid they'll fail. By broadcasting my goals, I had an additional incentive to achieve them.

Once you have set your goals and plans, review them often to see if you're on target. Keep accurate records. Analyze your performance and correct your mistakes. If you're having success, know what you're doing that's right, and keep on doing it.

Goals are dreams, and we all need them. Recently I saw a scrawny kid being interviewed by a sports commentator. "Look, there are more than a hundred thousand college basketball players out there competing against you, and many of them are taller and stronger than you. What makes you think you have a chance to make the pros?"

This awkward kid looked down at the ground for a moment to think. "I'll make the pros," he said softly. "It's been my dream since I can remember and nobody's going to take it away from me."

Well, he's got his dream—his goal; that's the first step toward success.

I've always dreamed about being the very best in whatever I did. At first, my dream was to be the best new agent for my company. Then I wanted to be the best in Lakeland; and after that I wanted to be the best in Central Florida; and then the whole state; and so on, until I dreamed about being the best in the whole world. I hope that I never run out of dreams. I like to quote Kahlil Gibran: "The significance of a man is not in what he attains but rather in what he longs to attain."

If you want something badly enough and the thought of it becomes firmly entrenched in your subconscious mind, soon everything you do is directed toward that goal. You'll find yourself automatically avoiding distractions and unproductive activity. You'll become "programmed" for success.

The Telephone as a Time-saving Tool

By now you know that I consider time to be my most valuable asset. And, as someone who constantly attempts to make the very best use of my time, I find the telephone to be my most valuable sales tool.

Although in some fields (e.g., the securities industry), an initial telephone call may result in a firm sale, I use the phone strictly to schedule appointments with new prospects. I want to give prospective clients an eyeball-to-eyeball sales presentation. By telephoning prospects I can cover much more ground than the person banging on doors. Having a long list of prospects is essential in scheduling appointments by telephone, particularly if you're making cold calls. On some days I'd go through thirty calls to get one solid commitment for an appointment. With a large list, I felt more secure, and that gave me confidence. I knew that when somebody said no, there were plenty of other prospects to call.

Many salespersons won't make cold calls because

they fear rejection. They take it personally and that's a mistake. When someone refused to see me, acted rudely, or hung up on me, I thought, "He can't be rejecting me, because he doesn't even know me." What risks are you taking when you make a cold call? You'll never get shot at or punched in the nose on the telephone. Once you know that nothing terrible can happen to you, it will be easier for you to make cold calls. If you get an appointment, great! If you don't . . . well, start dialing the next number.

In Chapter 4, I'll cover my telephone-sales approach. But for now, the most important thing for you to recognize is the value of the telephone as a tool for conserving time, energy, gasoline money, as well as wear and tear.

To recap, there's considerable thought and effort involved before a sales presentation. Success in the sales field depends upon more than a winning personality and a gift of gab. While the proverbial salesperson who can "sell refrigerators to the Eskimos" may indeed deliver a terrific sales presentation, he'd also better know what to do before the sale. If he doesn't, he'll never see enough Eskimos to sell those refrigerators to!

4

The Sales Approach

You only get one chance to make a first impression.
Be sure to make it a good one.

It's hogwash to say, "Don't judge a book by its
cover." Book publishers know that better than anyone.
Because people *do* judge books by their covers, publishers are willing to spend large sums of money on
them. And look at the thought that went into the pack-
aging of almost every product being offered to you.
Sometimes the package costs more than the product it
contains. Look at how carefully manufacturers choose
their media spokespeople. They know the importance
of a favorable first impression. In fact, every successful
person or company selling *any* product knows its value.

A first impression can open the door or close it; you
must get into a prospect's office or home if you hope to
make a sale. Remember the theory of ratios. The more
doors that slam in your face, the more doors you have
to bang on to get the numbers you need. Even further,
a strong first impression sets the stage for your presen-

tation. It permits you to start in a positive manner rather than having to fight an uphill battle with the prospect. Nobody wants to go to bat with two strikes before the first pitch.

Getting Past the Gatekeeper

It's common knowledge that many people are "on guard" when a salesperson approaches them. Many busy people protect themselves from salespeople with an intermediary. The buffer may be a secretary, a receptionist, an assistant, or a spouse. I call them the gatekeepers.

In order to be most effective with a gatekeeper, you must understand their job. First, let's assume that the decision-makers are generally the busiest people who place a high value on their time. To put it bluntly, there are too many ineffective salespeople out there hassling them. It's not possible for them to see everyone and still get their work done. However, everybody is dependent to some degree on salespeople. So, even a busy person will amicably agree to see *some* salespeople. It's up to the gatekeeper to determine *who* is given permission to go past the gate and enter the prospect's office. Obviously, if you're not good at getting past the gatekeeper, you're going to miss out on a lot of prospects who otherwise could have been sold.

If you worked for me I would insist that the purpose of the initial contact—either by phone or in person—would be strictly to make an appointment for a sales interview. Attempting to sell on the first call, I feel, implies lack of respect for the other guy's time. Your unexpected call may be interpreted as saying,

"Look here, Buster, I want to see you now, so drop everything and hear me out." Under no circumstances do you want to start off by appearing to be disrespectful to your prospect.

So secure an appointment for another time. You must keep this objective in mind when contacting the gatekeeper. And, since I guard my time so jealously, my first encounter with the gatekeeper is usually by telephone. However, if a situation requires an in-person call, my approach would be virtually identical.

On a cold call, when the secretary answers, "Mr. Smith's office," I first say, "Hello, this is Joe Gandolfo. Is he in?" There's no sense in saying more than I have to, and frequently I am put through to speak with the prospect.

Of course, it's not always so easy, and the gatekeeper often comes back with, "Does Mr. Smith know you?"

If it's a referral, which the vast majority of these calls have always been, I reply, "John Brown suggested that I call Mr. Smith. Kindly put me through to him." I answer her question politely and follow up by giving her a small command. By doing this, I am assuming that my answer to her question was satisfactory, and I *expect* now to be able to speak with Mr. Smith.

If I have not been referred to him, I say, "I've been seeing people in the automobile industry (or whatever business he's in) and I want to speak with Mr. Smith." And again, "Kindly put me through to him."

Often the gatekeeper will ask, "Whom do you represent?" or "What are you selling?" If this happens, I say, "I'm with ABC Company. Kindly put me through to him," or "I want to talk to him about his long-range investments and his life insurance program. Kindly put me through to him."

Generally, if you speak with conviction and confidence, the gatekeeper won't ask additional questions and your call will be put through. However, it's possible for the gatekeeper to say something like, "He's not interested" or "He has all the insurance he needs."

"Well, how do you know? Do you do the buying for him?" And again I say, "Kindly put me through to him."

If the gatekeeper again says, "He's not interested," I reply, "He's not? That's the first time in twenty-six years I ever heard that. What time does he usually get in the office?"

"I told you he doesn't talk to salesmen."

"I have to see him. I just want to meet somebody who has never talked to a salesman."

Generally, the gatekeeper doesn't know what to say at this point and my call is put through.

On the extremely difficult cases, the gatekeeper may say, "He's very busy now. Give me your phone number, and he'll call you."

"It's almost impossible to catch me. I'll call him back later. What time does he generally get into the office in the morning?" After I find out what time he first arrives in his office, that's when I call on him because it's a good opportunity to talk to him before he gets too busy.

On those rare occasions when I make a cold call in person, the gatekeeper might ask for my card. Some gatekeepers would read it and say, "Insurance? He's not interested in purchasing insurance."

"My time is very valuable, ma'am, and I wouldn't

come here if anybody else could do this important job for him. Please tell him that Joe Gandolfo is waiting to see him."

If the gatekeeper responds, "He's busy," I'll reply, "Please tell him that I will wait."

A technique I've used successfully was to call prospects who lived in a nearby community and tell the gatekeeper that I was calling long-distance. For some reason, there was always less resistance when it wasn't a local call. I suppose, for some, there's a sense of urgency connected to a long-distance call. Then, too, there are some people who believe that the out-of-towner is smarter than the local guy. Or maybe there's a mystique about people who come from faraway distances. Whatever, I was quick to tell many gatekeepers that I was calling from out of town. And as for those local ones to whom I couldn't get through the first time, I'd contact them again a week or so later while I was out of town by simply making a long-distance person-to-person call. Likewise, I would call prospects in my own hometown, the Lakeland area, and say, "I'm calling long-distance and wish to speak to. . . ." It's amazing how many gatekeepers lower their guard to the out-of-town caller.

Your approach to gatekeepers is important, so you must practice to get it down smoothly. Your time is too valuable to have a low batting average at this initial contact. While the gatekeeper may be a tough nut to crack, the prospect may be a piece of cake. There's a good reason that this is often the case. The prospect has trained his gatekeeper to weed out the good from the bad salespeople. With this in mind, he is conditioned to think that if you got through, then you must be worthy of a hearing. You'll often find that the tougher the gatekeeper, the better your reception with the prospect. The best salespeople are happy to find tough gatekeepers. They keep the weaker competition away!

The Initial Approach to a Prospect

Now that you're past the gatekeeper, and you get to speak to the prospect, what should you say?

First and foremost, don't forget that your only objective is to secure an appointment for a sales interview. It would be a serious faux pas to attempt anything else. *Under no circumstances should you ever attempt to sell at this stage.*

Whether you're in the prospect's office or have been put through to him on the telephone, your approach should be identical. Mine is, "Mr. Brown, I'm Joe Gandolfo with XYZ Company. Has Bill Smith mentioned my name to you?" (This breaks the ice, and it doesn't matter if he says yes or no.) "I don't want to take up your time today to discuss life insurance, but I would like to ask for an opportunity to meet with you sometime next week to share an idea with you that has been of help to other people in your field. Would next Thursday at two-thirty be convenient or would four be better?"

In the event that I don't have a referral, I use the name of one of the prospect's competitors who is already a client of mine: "Mr. Brown, has Fred Miller ever mentioned my name to you?" Now, it isn't likely that Miller, his competitor, would have talked to him about me; however, mentioning Miller is an icebreaker; and Brown is probably interested in knowing what his competitor is up to. The reaction with this approach is usually receptive and gets appointments.

Notice that I gave Brown a choice of two times to see me—at two-thirty or four next Thursday. Suggesting to see him the next week implies that I am a busy person. A prospect thinks, "Busy people are more successful than people who have a lot of time on their hands." It's also easier for a prospect to make a commitment to see a salesperson *next week*. He doesn't have to deal with it today and can cope better later. When a holiday is coming up soon, I say, "I don't want to talk with you today, but I do want to talk with you next week after the holiday." Apparently, this seems even farther into the future.

Giving him a choice of times for our meeting, rather than having him decide whether he wants to see me, is usually very effective. I have assumed that his only answer will be two-thirty or four. If he can't make one of those times, he'll come up with an alternate.

When I mention that I deal with his competition, it also tips him off that I am familiar with his problems. For the same reason, I might set up the appointment by saying, "I'd like to share an idea with you that's been of help to other auto dealers." He now thinks I am a specialist in his field; and secondly, it makes him feel like an oddball if he's not willing to discuss an idea that pertains to people in his field.

Again, *do not try to sell the prospect on your first call.* It is very poor strategy to attempt anything other than securing a future appointment. In my own office, I absolutely refuse to see anyone who walks in cold. I will see a salesperson only by appointment. The same thing applies to the salesperson who calls and tries to sell me over the telephone. He hasn't the slightest idea what he may be interrupting. I think it's just plain rude to interrupt another person.

Every now and then, there is the temptation to give an on-the-spot presentation, especially when a prospect says, "Say, Joe, what is it you want to tell me?" It used to be that my natural reaction was to go right into my sales talk. But I soon learned by experience that it would backfire. I could have kicked myself at those times.

Through trial and error, I discovered that it was far better to avoid giving on-the-spot presentations; and no matter how much a prospect pushed me to give him additional information, it worked much better when I'd say, "I'm sorry, but I have to rush, and it wouldn't be fair to either of us if I hurried through it right now. So, I'd like to be able to share my idea with you next Thursday."

Another approach I frequently use is: "My name is Joe Gandolfo. I am with XYZ Company. I didn't call you today to take up any of your time to discuss insurance, but I called to ask for an opportunity sometime next week to introduce myself personally and share an idea with you. If it fits with your philosophy and pocketbook, fine; if not, I promise you I'll be on my way. Can I see you next Thursday morning at seven, or would eight be better?"

On occasion, a prospect will say, "I'm just too busy to see you next week. In fact, I'm booked up for weeks. I don't have any openings in the foreseeable future." When a busy and successful person says this to me, I try to set an appointment with him before his normal workday begins. If he still can't figure out a time to see me, I say, "You have to eat sometime. How about breakfast? Six-thirty, okay?" Successful people like to do business with other hardworking people who also get up early. But if I can't pin him down to an early-morning time, I'll try for lunch. I might also add, "I'm on call twenty-four hours a day, so you give me a time that's convenient with you and I'll work it into my schedule." Does it work? More than 50 percent of my sales have been made before nine in the morning. That tells you something doesn't it?

Selling Yourself

No matter what product you sell, never forget that *you've got to sell yourself!* In today's highly competitive marketplace, practically no salesperson has such a monopoly that the customer is forced to say, "I can't stand the salesperson, but he's the only one I could buy from." In my field, there are more than 1,800 insurance companies, and not a single one has an exclusive product. With multiple listings today, every real-estate agent in town has the same property portfolio. A Merrill Lynch broker sells the same stocks as the Dean Witter and Bache representatives. The Xerox copier salesperson's product might not be so different from IBM's or Eastman Kodak's. And IBM's word processor might not differ a great deal from Lanier's or Wang's. The most significant difference that determines which product is bought is the *salesperson*.

Now, I'm not going to go into any details about the obvious—your appearance. As I stated at the beginning of this chapter, you get only one chance to make a first impression, so naturally I advocate being well-groomed and properly dressed. I'm a stickler for neatness. I strongly suggest having a clean car, clean fingernails, a good shine on your shoes—the whole nine yards. That's all I'll say about appearance, because there are lots of books that can tell you everything about the subject that common sense doesn't dictate.

When does a salesperson begin to sell himself? *Before* the sale of the product. I quickly identify myself by doing a little tooting of my own horn. "Mr. Prospect," I say in a modest tone, "in many circles I'm considered to be the number-one life insurance agent in the world. I've been written up in the *Wall Street Journal, Fortune, Forbes,* and several other publications. I was selected as the world's top life insurance agent in the best-selling book *Ten Greatest Salespersons.*" At this point I put my business card down on the table and say, "There are more than four hundred thousand life insurance agents and financial counselors on the face of this earth, and I think it's important that you know about my qualifications. If you'll permit me, I'd like to tell you something about myself. . . ."

I continue until I'm convinced that he's impressed. Then finally I say, "Over ninety percent of all men and women with whom I have done business have *continued* doing business with me. I'm interested in a long and enduring relationship."

I have plenty of credentials to rattle off now; but in my early days, I'd tell a prospect that I was on schedule for the Million Dollar Round Table, that I was becoming a CLU, that I was a member of the National Association of Life Underwriters, and that I belonged to my company's President's Club.

What am I doing? I'm selling myself to my prospect. I want him to know that I'm a conscientious, hard worker. He should know that I'm very good at what I do. And I'm telling him that I will be around in the business for a long, long time.

In recent years, when my secretaries send out a letter confirming my appointment with a prospect, they include a brochure about me—a tool used to pre-sell me. It contains about the same information that I used to tell prospects before I began my presentation. I believe you should make up a brochure about yourself to mail out to your prospects and clients. Most important, the brochure should be about *who you are*, not about your product and your company. You can include another brochure about your product and your company, but let the prospect know about you as an individual— what kind of person you are. If you haven't yet had great success in the business world, tell the prospect about your goals and how you intend to accomplish them. Or tell him about your personal achievements.

Today, when a client visits my office, I have many awards and honors on my wall, again telling a story about me—selling Joe Gandolfo. While other companies put up outdoor billboards to promote themselves, I use my wall space for the same purpose. I get a kick out of watching a client study my plaques when I have to excuse myself from the office for a few moments. And that's exactly why they're there. I want him to know I've worked very hard to get so much recognition in my industry.

If you don't have awards and honors to decorate your office walls, put up photos of your family, personal recognition from such organizations as your church, college, the Boy Scouts, Chamber of Commerce, and so on. What's most important is that you take advantage of this wall space and use it to toot your horn to your captive audience.

Doctors line their walls with various degrees they've collected as undergraduates, medical students, residents, and interns. Those degrees tell the patient an important message: "I am a qualified physician. Your life is safe in my hands." Some people decorate their office walls and the effect backfires on them. I remember once visiting a car salesman's office where the wall had photographs of many different car models, including sports cars that he didn't sell. As I looked at the different cars, I began to think that perhaps I'd enjoy a sports car more than the sedan I came in to see! A real-estate office I visited was decorated with mounted heads of moose and deer. I thought that, to many people, killing these animals for sport would be a real turnoff. In another office, large mounted fish lined the walls. I'm sure that the walls distracted him, because instead of selling me on his product, this salesman told a boring story about a large sailfish. Use those walls to promote yourself—don't simply decorate them!

Sharing an Idea

One of my key phrases is, "I want to share an idea." This phrase is the focal point of my approach, and through my entire career I have never deviated from it. It's simple and direct: "I didn't call today to discuss life insurance with you but to ask for an opportunity to get together sometime next week to share an idea with you." It's difficult for almost anyone to turn down the opportunity to share an idea, so no matter what product is being sold, this approach works.

Every now and then, however, there is a prospect who will say, "No I'm not interested." When I hear this, my stock reply is, "John, may I ask you a question before I hang up?" And out of courtesy the prospect will say, "Sure, what's your question?"

"If you'll recall, I said I wanted to share an idea with you. Well, you know the value of the U.S. Patent Office, don't you?"

"Yes."

"Well, believe it or not, during the John Quincy Adams administration, Congress came within three votes of killing it! They believed that all of the good ideas had been conceived, and wanted to save the taxpayers' money. Since then, of course, we've had radios, automobiles, motion pictures, television, computers, spaceships to the moon, and who knows what all, even in your own business. The question I would like to ask before I hang up is, *Have you closed your patent office?*"

"Er, no, Joe, not if you look at it that way."

"Fine. May I see you next Thursday?"

This approach has generated millions and millions of dollars of extra sales for me. I recommend that you try it—it's dynamite.

Selling the Decision-Maker

For obvious reasons, you want to give your sales presentation to the individual with the authority to make a buying decision. It's futile to do otherwise, because you can't make a sale if the person you're selling to isn't in a position to say yes. Nothing is more frustrating than to give a sales presentation and then be told, "Thanks for telling me about it. It's a wonderful product. I'll explain it to Mrs. Williams who's responsible for buying widgets in our company." *Don't ever count on anyone selling your product for you.* You've got to make your appointment with the decision-maker. That's all there is to it!

After the prospect has given you an appointment, cover yourself. "Mr. Green, I want you to be sure to include at our meeting any persons you believe are necessary to effect a decision." Suggest his CPA or attorney or comptroller if you think it's necessary, or have them all present. Now you've set the stage for your closing. He can't procrastinate when you ask for a decision.

Early in my career I realized the importance of having the decision-maker present. There were many times when a husband would say at the end of my sales presentation, "It sounds good to me, but I have to talk it over with my wife." In the meantime, I had spent an hour and a half with the prospect in his home, and all this time his wife had been in the other room watching television, knitting, or cleaning the kitchen. I could have kicked myself for not inviting her in to hear my presentation. I learned the hard way that you must ask the prospect to have his wife present if she is to be sharing in the decision-making. If he'd say she wasn't going to be involved, I'd reply, "It's good to meet a person who can make a decision on his own." This remark would make him feel good about himself, and it would eliminate procrastination at the close of the sale.

The same approach works when I talk to business

people at large companies. If a prospect says he's the decision-maker, I say, "It's good to meet a person who's capable of making a decision on his own without a committee." Generally, this remark puts a prospect in a position where he will not want to disappoint me at the close by feebly admitting he can't make a decision on his own. It's best to find out up front.

Thus, your approach is vital because it sets the stage for your sales presentation. And remember: If you don't get past the gatekeeper, you can't possibly make a sale. Super-important is that, during your initial sales approach, your prime objective is to set up an appointment. Nothing more. Make sure, if at all possible, that all the decision-makers will be there. And finally, the two best things to sell are ideas and yourself.

5

Selling Is 98% Understanding Human Beings . . . 2% Product Knowledge

Several years ago, I wrote a book titled *Selling is 98% Understanding Human Beings . . . 2% Product Knowledge.* Some people, who I don't think got past the title, accused me of putting down product knowledge. These people obviously didn't understand me, and probably don't understand other human beings!

Of course you need product knowledge! No one knows that better than I. Although I'm one of the most successful salesmen in my field, I still study an average of two hours a day. I'm formally educated in my business as well as self-educated. I didn't study life insurance at the Wharton School of Business, become a Chartered Life Underwriter and a Chartered Financial Counselor without knowing my product inside and out. I earned an MBA and a Ph.D. from California University. So, when I say product knowledge contributes about 2 percent to the sale, it's not because I don't understand the value of product knowledge—*it's because I know my business!* And I'm willing to share with you what I know.

However, as important as it is to know your product thoroughly, understanding human beings is what selling is really all about. There are thousands of professors who are experts in computers, real estate, insurance, and many other products, who, if they had to depend on selling those products for a living, would starve. The same applies to the thousands of product experts who work behind desks in their small offices for large corporations across the country. So, while it's necessary to know your product, it's even more important that you *understand human beings.*

The Warm-Up

I never approach a prospect with any preconceived ideas about what to sell him. And the only way I know what the customer wants or needs is by asking a lot of questions. It doesn't make sense for a life insurance agent to attempt to sell a policy without knowing all about the prospect. I've got to know such things as: How much insurance does he now have? (Maybe he's overinsured.) What can he afford? What are his family's needs? How old is he? What's his health like? What's his occupation? These are just a few of dozens of questions I must have answers for so I can tailor-make an insurance program for him.

A salesperson can't assume anything until he asks enough questions to understand the customer's wants and needs. This is true even when a customer walks into an automobile dealership to buy a car. He shouldn't try to push a black four-door on a prospect simply because that's the car he wants to move on that particular day. A stockbroker shouldn't sell Widgets, Inc., stock to every one of his clients because his company is underwriting a new offering of four million shares. Nor should a retail furniture salesperson try to sell an Early American bedroom set to every customer who walks into his bedding department. No salesperson should attempt to sell his product until he knows what the prospect wants.

So I begin every sales presentation with my "warm-up" session. I start off by saying "John, before I get started on the idea that I want to share with you, I have to ask you some questions." Now, keep in mind that I have already identified myself, giving him an extensive review of my qualifications. By letting him know in advance who I am, he knows that I am well-qualified to ask confidential questions. Since I will be asking questions about his net worth and annual earnings, I preface the warm-up session by saying, "John, my role is that of a physician who examines you. Now, if I find something wrong , maybe I'll write a prescription. If it fits your philosophy and pocketbook, fine. If not, as I promised you when I called for an appointment, I'll be on my way. Fair enough?" Then I start asking questions.

"Do you have any strong feelings about life insurance?" I ask, and give him lots of time to respond.

"What financial formula did you use to arrive at the amount of life insurance you now have?"

"What is your feeling about life insurance as an investment?"

"Have you developed a particular attitude about life insurance providing only protection?"

"What do you think about life insurance as a means of saving money for the education of your children?"

"What is your opinion of life insurance as a source of retirement income?"

"Do you have any thoughts on mortgage insurance?"

"Do you have life insurance on your wife?"

"What about your children?"

"Do you have any key-man insurance in your corporation?"

"How do you feel about pension plans using life insurance?"

"What is your feeling about using life insurance as liquid dollars to pay federal estate taxes?"

These are just a few of the questions I ask to get the prospect thinking—and talking. Later my questions get more confidential. For example, I might ask a married man, "Do you have a good marriage?"

"Do you run around?"

"Are you hiding money anywhere?"

"Do you take money out of your business without declaring it?"

As you can see, I ask question after question; and I sit back and let my prospect talk. And I *listen*.

A while back I walked into an auto dealership. I wasn't in there more than a few minutes, and the salesman tried to sell me one of his models in the showroom. He didn't ask me anything about myself or what kind of car I might like to drive. Although I was in the market for a new car, I walked out very disgusted. I had a certain model and color in mind, but he never attempted to find out what I wanted. I went to another dealer, and he asked me all kinds of questions.

"How many are there in your family, Joe?"

"What ages are your kids?"

"How many miles do you drive a year?"

"How important is gas mileage to you?"

"Do you prefer a two-door or four-door?"

"What colors do you like?"

The salesman asked me all kinds of questions, and he ended up selling me a car. I walked out of there feeling very good. I had spent a lot of money, but I felt that I was getting the right car for me.

A good real-estate agent will do the same thing. He doesn't take a prospect for a ride in his car and show every home in the community listed for sale. He'll ask lots of questions and then select the homes on the market that might interest the buyer.

"How many children do you have?"

"How old are they and what grades are they in?"

"Do you like to do yard work?"

"Are you and your family outdoors people?"

"Do you mind driving a long distance to work, or do you prefer to live close by?"

"Do you have a dog?"

"How important is it to your family that you be in a particular school district?"

"Do you like modern homes, Early American style [etc.]?"

"How important is a large yard to your family?"

"Do you like a ranch-style or two-floor plan?"

"In what price range is the home you are looking for?"

Again, the salesperson conducts a question-and-answer session to find out what the customer wants. It doesn't matter what your product is, you've got to find out what the prospect wants or needs before you can sell him. If you fail to do this, you'll not only be operating in the dark, but you're signaling to him that you don't care. If you're not already conducting a question-and-answer session, go ahead and try it. You'll be pleasantly surprised by the reaction it generates.

"How did you ever get into your field?" I ask this question of everyone. They thoroughly enjoy talking about their careers and I genuinely enjoy listening to their replies. It fascinates me to hear how successful people got their start in business, and every time I ask this question, I learn something that helps me sell.

Now, a final word about the warm-up session: Before you begin asking a lot of questions, you must do your homework so you ask the *right questions*. To know the right questions to ask a business person, you must study his industry in detail. You must understand the kinds of problems he faces; and by your questions, he will recognize that you do. Imagine going to a doctor with a bum back, and he didn't ask you any questions about where it hurt? Instead, he just said, "I'll give you some pills, and if it still hurts, come back and see me in a week." Then, after he wrote out a prescription, he said, "See my receptionist on your way out to make your next appointment with me."

I don't think you'd have much confidence in this doctor.

However a good doctor will ask dozens of detailed questions before making a decision on how to treat you. "Tell me where it hurts," he asks.

"Mmm, does it hurt when I press on this spot?"

"When did you first begin to notice it?"

"What were you doing at the time?"

"Does it hurt when you move your arm like this? How about like this?"

"Will you walk over there? Now stand and bend slightly. Okay, now sit down. Sit up straight. Do you always sit leaning over like that?" the doctor patiently asks.

After asking many questions, he finally says, "Okay, now here's what I recommend. . . ."

It's more likely that this is the kind of doctor you put your faith in—and the one to whom you are willing to trust your life or perhaps that of a loved one. As I have mentioned, like the doctor, you have to probe.

The Art of Listening

Of all our communication skills, listening is the most overlooked. And that's an incredible mistake. Every school teaches us reading, writing, and oral skills, but I've never seen a school course in listening. It's no wonder that we have so many interpersonal problems—misunderstandings, divorces, generation gaps. We're a population of talkers and very few listeners. And many salespeople are among the worst offenders!

They believe that if they can get through their presentation nonstop, without any interruptions from the prospect, a sale is certain to follow. Some are taught this when they first break into sales. They are given a canned pitch from which they never stray. These pitches don't allow the customer in—they become the ultimate in one-way communication. Too often a person with this kind of training grows up to believe that he must dominate the customer, never allowing him to contribute to the sale. And too often this salesperson develops into a flimflam artist who has no respect for his prospect, who tries to make the sale by browbeating, intimidation, and coercion . . . anything but two-way communication.

Too many salespeople think this is the way to go. They believe that the more proficient they get at ramming a sale through, the richer they will get. *They are all wet.* They are doomed to be small potatoes all their lives. Most will wander from deal to deal, sometimes on the verge of making a kill but barely making a living. A realistic profile of the highly successful salesperson would include, in its image, an individual who asks a lot of questions—and then sits back and listens. Every great salesperson I've ever met fits this description. I can also think of an army of potentially successful salespeople who just missed because they didn't sharpen their listening skills. How many couples have you seen who never stop talking *at* each other—often talking at the same time with neither hearing what the other has to say! Sometimes we need to be silent, to absorb what's being said, to gather our thoughts. It's sad for people to treat silence in conversation as undesirable. Frankly, I welcome it as an opportunity for each party to think.

People who insist on dominating a conversation rarely hear what the other person has to say. Their minds are always preoccupied with what to say! That happens too often in a sales interview. If the salesperson would only learn to shut up and listen, the customer will invariably tell what his problems are and give clues on how to sell to him. In my own case, my clients do considerably more talking than I. After I ask a question, I shut up; I let my client talk. If he doesn't reply, I patiently sit still and wait for him to speak. I don't feel threatened by the silence—I wait for an answer. Too often, after a question is asked and a prospect pauses to reflect, the salesperson can't stand it—so he either answers his own question or asks another one. You've got to let the prospect talk. Let him tell you what's on his mind.

It's like the old story about the patient who asks his psychiatrist, "How come you always answer with a question?"

The psychiatrist replies, "What do you mean?"

It can be downright offensive to the other person when you don't let him express himself. More than likely he'll resent it, and even if he wants your product, he won't want to buy it from you. Remember that everybody loves to hear the sound of his own voice. And, for the most part, the prospect loves to talk. So let him. Your job is to guide him with the right questions and let him come to his own conclusion that he should buy your product.

Another thing happens when you don't permit the prospect to speak. He begins to feel that he's not in control of making the buying decision but, instead, it's being made for him. He then begins to feel pressured and uncomfortable. Next he begins to resist you. He finally begins to search for reasons not to buy from you—and you have lost the sale!

An observant salesperson will hear many clues that typically go unnoticed by the nonlistener. These buying signals are often the "hot buttons" that must be known in order to make the sale. For example, a car

buyer might say, "The price of gas is simply outra-
geous today," which signals to the salesperson that he
should sell a low-maintenance model with good gas
mileage. A real-estate agent who listens carefully hears
a young doctor say, "My wife's a professor at the university." This may be a tip that a home in a good
school district is a top priority to them. An astute
stockbroker is alerted to a client's remark when he
says, "My earnings last year were in the high six figures, but I can't accumulate any money." The broker
recognizes this to mean that the client is more interested in growth stocks than high-income-yielding investments, and he gears his sales presentation to this
knowledge. No matter what product you sell, your
prospect will tell you what he wants so you can make
the sale—but you've got to *listen.*

Showing the Customer That You Care

When you listen to what your customer has to say,
you're demonstrating that you care about him. When
speaking to him, you must always look squarely into his
eyes; and when you listen, you should be looking at his
lips. Never take your eyes off him. Even as you reply,
just nod your head and keep your eyes firmly fixed on
him. This eye contact is vital, and it shows that you
sincerely care about him.

In my opinion, nothing is more offensive than a
salesperson who doesn't give his undivided attention
to a client during a sales presentation. What do you
imagine your client is going to think if you're in his
house and have your eyes glued on his good-looking
wife or daughter? Or when you're in his office and an

attractive secretary walks by, and you're staring at her legs? Or your eyes are fixed on the pretty waitress during a luncheon meeting? Your eyes are telling him that you're more interested in looking at women than you are in talking to him. You're signaling that you really don't care about him—he's not as important as they are.

When you're talking to a client but not giving him your complete, undivided attention, he is thinking, "I am the most important human being here, and unless you pay attention to me, I don't care what you're selling —even if you're giving it away—I don't want it." Remember that not only do you communicate to him verbally, but nonverbally with your eye contact, facial expressions, and body language. If you're not completely sincere, he senses it by your nonverbal communication. You can't fake it—unless you have his best interests at heart, you won't come across as a trustworthy person.

A chemistry exists when two people meet eyeball-to-eyeball, and if you are a good, caring person, the other will know it. He will sense that you are at peace with yourself. The mental gymnastics that go on in his mind are, "I trust this person, and I know that he is right with himself and his God. He will not mistreat me nor lie to me, and therefore he is the person I want to do business with." Every super-successful salesperson that I've met comes across as a thoughtful, loving, caring individual who knows inner peace. It's a tough image to fake!

Often, salespeople give me excuses for not selling well: "Oh, my price is too high." Or "My competition does this or that, and we don't." Or "Our production is all screwed up." Everything and everybody is blamed—it was their manager's fault, something technical went wrong, and so on. They aren't being honest and sincere with their prospects, with themselves, or with me.

You've got to project sincerity and put the customer's interests first. Study successful people. Their customers *always* come first. With this approach, the money automatically comes. But when money is put first, success is usually a long way down the road.

Now and then a salesperson will tell me that he has tried my warm-up session, but it doesn't work well for him. "The prospect won't respond when I ask him questions. He especially resents my asking personal questions and won't open up to me." In such cases, the problem generally is that the salesperson lacks conviction. His questions come across as routine and rote. No real interest is projected, no sincerity, and the customer feels it!

How many times has a salesperson walked into a prospect's office and given an insincere compliment? It's as if he were trained to start off his presentation by always making a flattering remark. For instance, he might say, "Hey, that's really beautiful wallpaper," or "Say, I really love that photograph of your daughter." It would serve him right if the prospect responded, "That's not my daughter—that's my wife." I think most people resent a salesperson who makes this kind of small talk, especially at the very beginning of a sales interview. The prospect's time is valuable, and he's not interested in phony compliments—he wants to get down to business and find out *what you can do for him!*

Believing in Your Own Product

A salesperson has to believe in his product a hundred percent. Do you know that before I owned a million-dollar policy on my own life, I had a difficult time selling one to anyone else! Then, when I owned one, it became easy for me to talk to somebody else about his having that much life insurance. The same thing was true with selling tax shelters. Once I began putting my money into tax shelters, I had no problem convincing other people to put their money into them.

There's something about it when somebody asks, "Say, Joe, are you in it?" and I respond, "Yeah, I've got my money in it too." That conviction does wonders for persuading the other guy.

The same thing applies to salespeople in other fields. A Buick salesman would make a serious blunder if he drove an Oldsmobile. A clothing salesman in a fine men's store would have a difficult time convincing his customer to purchase an expensive suit if he wore a cheap one.

Of course, there are instances when a salesperson isn't expected to own the product he sells. A Rolls Royce buyer doesn't expect a salesperson to be able to afford a $100,000 Silver Cloud. In fact, he might be offended if a salesperson did! Likewise, a customer doesn't expect a salesperson to own an $8 million jet or a $10 million computer. A doctor isn't expected to have had a hernia to know how to treat one, nor is the pharmacist supposed to have taken every drug that he dispenses. But with most products, I strongly recommend that you do use what you sell.

Two Pet Peeves

I have two pet peeves that drive me up a wall. One, I can't believe the stupidity of salespeople who smoke when they are working. My objection is strictly business-related, so don't get the impression that I'm preaching.

There's nothing more offensive to me than when a salesperson lights up a cigarette and pollutes the air I'm breathing. In my opinion, he's guilty of extreme rudeness to me or anyone else. It doesn't matter if he asks, "Do you mind if I smoke?" In most cases, the prospect does mind, but out of courtesy he'll give his consent. The point is, the smoker never knows when he's offending. I'll even go one step further. Even when the prospect smokes, I think it's wrong for the salesperson to smoke during a sales presentation. Smoking is distracting because the smoker's hands are always busy, and the prospect might worry that he'll drop a hot ash on his desk or carpeting, and the distraction will cause the salesperson to lose eye contact with the prospect.

My second pet peeve is the use of alcohol in any situation where a client might be involved. Obviously, the worst possible scenario would be for you to walk into someone's office after a couple of shots. And I advise you not to drink with a client—even if he's belting down one drink after another.

I'll go one step further and recommend that you refrain from drinking in public places where your clients might see you. I don't drink alcoholic beverages, so I don't have to avoid doing this; but if you use them, drink at home or in the privacy of someone's home. I believe a professional person has an obligation to behave in a professional manner twenty-four hours a day, seven days a week. This advice applies to doctors, lawyers, politicians, government employees, CPAs, and anyone else who has a confidential relationship with clients. After all, wouldn't it make you feel a bit uncomfortable if you saw your doctor or lawyer out getting plastered? There's no place for it in your career, not if you want to project a truly professional image. Not if you want to be a real success.

Sometimes I'm asked, "Come on now, Joe, not even a few drinks at the club with the guys?" My answer is always no. I don't think your clients want you to be "one of the boys." As a professional salesman in whom they confide very personal information, you wouldn't want to be seen boozing it up. This may mean sacrificing a personal pleasure; but as I said before, there are certain prices to be paid if you want to be a top-money-making salesperson.

"May I Make a Suggestion?"

Throughout this book I emphasize again and again that you must always put the customer's interests above everything else. I have learned early in my career that you sell people what *they* want or need. It doesn't make any difference that you have only the black model in the showroom. If he wants something else, that's what you sell him. And it doesn't matter that your company has a sales contest in progress that's pushing Model Number 504 this week; if he wants Model Number 800, that's what you sell him.

Many insurance agents don't like to sell term insurance because the low premiums generate low commissions. So when a client calls for term insurance, they insist on selling him whole life and often lose the sale. If my client wants term insurance, that's exactly what I sell. When I do this, he thinks, "Joe was so smart the first time when he sold me what I thought was best that he can come back now and sell me anything he wants." So, later I go back and sell him whole life insurance. On the other hand, if the prospect thinks you're only interested in selling him what you want—for the commissions—he'll have no confidence that you will be around to give him service later on. It's important to recognize that there are many more sales after the initial one, but you only get them if you treat the customer right the first time. Repeat business is the real gravy in selling, and the one-shot salespeople never last long enough to enjoy it.

There are two exceptions when I'll sell my client what *I* think is best for him. First is when he asks for my advice: "Joe, what do you think I should buy? I'm open to suggestions."

Second, if I feel he's making a poor decision, I'll say, *"May I make a suggestion?"* It doesn't matter what you sell. These are magic words: *May I make a suggestion?* After all, who's going to say, "No, you can't make a suggestion." Once he says okay, I tell him what I think is best for him.

This is it: you've got to know your product, but above all else, you must understand your customer. The best way to understand somebody is to listen to what he has to say. Ask dozens and dozens of questions in getting to know your client. And, most important, keep quiet and let him do most of the talking. Don't assume that you have to dominate the sales presentation—give your prospect an ample opportunity to talk. When you listen, you demonstrate that you care about him. Always remember that, during the sales presentation, you must give your full, undivided attention to your prospect. This is *his* time, and he's your number-one priority.

Some final advice: if you're a novice salesperson, be patient. It takes time to really get to understand human beings, and that knowledge can't be obtained in the classroom. You gain it through experience. And again, the salesperson who sees a thousand prospects in a year's time will have four times as much experience as the one who sees 250 prospects during the same period. The more experience you have, the more you will understand the people you depend on.

6

Selling the Concept

The words *selling* and *persuading* are generally used as if they were synonyms. Webster and Roget may agree with that, but I don't. If you are going to sell the way I do and be as successful at it as I am, you will have to master a lot more than the art of persuasion. I've covered a few facets of successful selling; now here's another—and, believe me, it's important: To make it big, you have to be a *creative, resourceful "idea man."*

There are four hundred thousand life insurance agents covering this country. Their insurance policies are basically the same as mine, but I'm not competing with them. I'd be a fool to knock heads with an army of four hundred thousand. Do you know why I'm not competing with them? Because they are pounding the pavement selling *complicated, legalistic insurance policies*, while I'm selling *ideas, concepts, and solutions to problems*. From my very first approach to the signing of the contract, I sell ideas. Remember my approach? No matter who the prospect may be, I start off by saying

95

the same thing to everyone: "I don't want to take up your time today to discuss life insurance, but I would like to ask for an opportunity to meet with you sometime next week to *share an idea* with you." I've been using this same approach for years, and it works today just as well as ever. I don't sell insurance, I sell ideas.

Concept-selling will work for *you*, no matter what your product is—tangible or intangible. Once understood and mastered, it works like magic. The top producers in every industry sell concepts, not products; that's why they are the top producers—it's no coincidence.

I don't try to sell legal documents with nonforfeiture options, settlement options, and automatic premium loans. If I did that, not only would I totally confuse people and bore them silly, but even worse, I'd slow down the whole decision-making process! Actually, when you analyze an insurance policy, the document is a written contract between two parties whereby the first party agrees to pay to the other a specific amount of money each year, for which the second party will pay a specific sum in the event of the first party's death according to the financial obligations of each party which are determined by certain mortality tables based on the life expectancy of the insured at the time of the execution of the contract—unless the insured's health and occupational hazards do not conform with certain standards, and adjustment increases the rates. . . .

Should I continue, or am I losing you already?

I quit selling insurance policies years ago and stopped thinking of myself as an "insurance man." Since then, I've helped my clients with their financial planning. Now, it's true that my client may still end up owning a legal document insuring his life, but it's my ideas he buys, not the actual instrument.

For instance, the thirty-five-year-old man with a wife and three children who purchases a $200,000 life insurance policy is buying peace of mind. The money will provide his family with an annuity that would replace his lost earnings if he should die while they're still young. He's fulfilling his responsibilities as a father and husband.

In another case, two business partners may buy the same $200,000 life insurance policy on each other's life in what is known as a buy-sell agreement. Basically, the policies are purchased to provide a fixed amount of money so the surviving partner can acquire the deceased partner's ownership interest from his surviving heirs. Again I am selling a concept, the solution to a possible catastrophe. In most cases, life insurance is the *only* solution, because it wouldn't be otherwise possible for the surviving partner to raise enough money to buy out the interest of the deceased partner's heirs. Likewise, the heirs are able to avoid being silent partners in a business that they may not choose to own.

Then, in yet another case, that $200,000 life insurance might be the most feasible way for the survivors of the deceased to have enough cash on hand to pay estate taxes. This need is met by informing a wealthy individual of the amount of taxes his estate will be obligated to pay in the event of his death. He must be made aware of the financial perils that would arise if his heirs were forced to liquidate assets in a depressed market in order to pay those taxes.

As you can see, there are numerous ways to sell

concepts rather than life insurance policies. In the preceding three examples, the product was exactly the same. However, each time the sale was made by selling a different concept. In my warm-up session, I ask dozens and dozens of questions, always probing to see where the need for a life insurance product may exist. When the need becomes evident to the client, I make the sale.

One of my best approaches to wealthy people is through a brochure I mail out. It states, "If you're paying more than $4,000 a year in taxes, you're paying too much." It's a great opening for selling tax shelters—and, again, I'm selling a concept. When people respond to the brochure, it's not because they are interested in investing in an oil well, in real estate, or in a piece of equipment with a lease-back agreement. They want to pay less tax! The product they might buy from me is incidental, a means to that end.

Recently I talked to a real-estate broker about why people invest in orange groves. "Some people might like the tax-shelter aspects of an orange grove," the broker remarked, "and another person may think it has appreciation potential. Still another person may want to live on it, and another buys it because it feeds his ego. He enjoys bragging about it at cocktail parties. 'I own an orange grove.'"

There are many reasons for buying a shopping center or an apartment complex or an expensive automobile. What turns on your prospect? The best way to find out is by asking enough questions and listening.

Take a look at the computer industry. Buck Rogers, IBM's vice-president of marketing, says, "We simply supply a solution to our customers' problems.

"For example, if I walk into your office and say, 'I've got something that's going to make your job easier, reduce your cost, and allow you to give better service to your customer,' you're going to be interested in hearing what I've got to tell you. *And that's what it's all about!*"

Other office-equipment manufacturers also sell what their product can do. Typewriter and copy-machine companies sell products that make crisp images in addition to saving time and making work easier. Dictating-equipment companies sell convenience—their product saves time and makes things easier for the operator. Nobody sells little black boxes (or whatever color the machine happens to be). Instead, they sell concepts: what the machine will do for the prospect.

A while back, a man called me and said he wanted to stop by and share an idea. It was a new retailing concept that would save me considerable time and offer me convenience. I was impressed with his professional approach on the telephone, so I consented to meet with him.

When Michael David entered my office, I was impressed by his appearance. Dressed in a three-piece pin-striped suit, he was spic and span from head to foot. "Mr. Gandolfo, I'm Michael David with The Image Group," he said, "and I know how valuable your time is, so I'll get right down to business. The Image Group is a custom tailor of fine men's suits; and our clientele are busy executives like you who don't have a whole lot of time to shop. And, like you, these gentlemen are discriminating about their appearance. What we do, sir, is bring the tailoring shop directly to the executive's office. We have the finest tailoring, the world's best fabrics, and an enormous selection. If I may, Mr. Gandolfo, I would like to show you some of our fabrics."

I nodded that he had my permission, and as he opened his leather briefcase, he mentioned several of his prominent customers whom I knew personally. He also asked me if I liked the way they dressed, and I said, "Very much so."

While flipping through dozens of swatches, he said, "We can offer you any style suit you want. Natural shoulder, three-buttoned, two-buttoned, wide or narrow belt loops, pleated or nonpleated pants—you name it and we'll make it exactly the way you want it. We also tailor the suit exactly to your dimensions, Mr. Gandolfo. . . . What size coat do you wear?"

"Forty-two."

"And your waist?"

"Thirty."

"As you know, you can't find ready-made suits in your size with a thirty-inch waist," he said, marking down my measurements as he talked. "A typical men's store stocks only a handful of suits in size forty-two, but look at the selection we can offer you. We have hundreds of patterns, and there are dozens of different styles that we make them up in. When you stop to think about it, we have a selection of literally thousands of suits, don't we, Mr. Gandolfo?"

I nodded, and he knew that he had me. "And do me a favor, Michael," I replied. "Quit calling me Mr. Gandolfo. The name is Joe."

"Do you mind if I ask you a few questions, Joe?" he asked politely. "Tell me about your existing wardrobe.

What patterns and colors of suits do you have now?"

He kept quiet as I described my suits to him. As I spoke, he wrote everything down on a yellow legal pad.

"You have a very nice wardrobe," he commented. "Which color of these pinstripe patterns do you think you'd like to add to your existing suits?"

He handed a book of swatches to me and remained silent. I studied them and replied, "This one looks really nice. . . ."

"Let me take your measurements, Joe," he said, taking out his tape. He then measured me in great detail. "I promise you, Joe, you'll never have a suit fit as fine as this one. And once you've bought a suit from The Image Group, you'll never want to buy another one from anyone else. By the way, once we make up the first suit, we keep your measurements on file so we won't have to take the time to measure you again."

I ended up buying a suit from him then, and several more on subsequent calls. When I analyzed why I buy from this company, I concluded that it is the great concept I buy, not the suits. The concept that appeals to me is the time-saving feature, along with being offered a much larger selection. All in all, it makes buying a suit from The Image Group a very pleasant experience—something that formerly had been a hassle.

You can learn a lot about selling ideas and concepts by looking outside the direct-sales field. Some incredibly successful businesses developed through the process of concept-selling.

The mail-order business today is, by some estimates, a $50 billion industry. Why is it so successful? It's not because they sell you something you can't buy at your local store. So if it's not the products they sell, then what is it? With so many women entering the job market, buying patterns have drastically changed in America. A mail-order company fulfills a need by offering convenience to the person who can't find the time to store-shop—a terrific idea, which has proven successful. Although the mail-order industry has been around for more than a hundred years, the convenience concept has never had such an important impact on the American public. According to some experts, the mail-order business in America has just scratched the surface.

Did you ever watch those Ford Motor Company television commercials? They show a demonstration that has a microphone just outside the car and another one on the inside. They roll up the windows and show you how quiet it is inside. They're selling the idea of a more quiet ride; but to the best of my knowledge, it's always going to be quieter when the windows are rolled up.

A man once told me that he bought a life insurance policy from an agent because, if he got hurt or sick, he wouldn't have to pay the premium. Again, a concept was sold. The agency was smart and didn't tell him that 1,800 other insurance companies offer the same thing with a waiver-of-premium rider. He didn't tell the man that he was selling a disability income policy along with the life insurance policy—and the income paid by the company when he was disabled would cover the life insurance policy's premium. Instead, the agent told him, "If you become disabled, we'll pay the premiums for you."

Now let's consider the home computer. In a recent

television commercial, the pitch was: "The computer is the wave of the future. Anyone who isn't computer-oriented will become obsolete. Be sure to buy a home computer so your child can get the necessary exposure—if you fail to, his future will be limited." Their concept, for what it's worth, is based on the fear that any family without a home computer would be neglecting their children—a failure bordering on child abuse!

Another example of great concept-selling is the no-frills airlines that have come into existence during the past few years. While the giant airlines are losing a great deal of money, the new economy carriers are operating with healthy profits. People Express Airlines is a shining example of concept-selling. They don't simply sell flights from one city to another. They sell value. Their ads say, "It's cheaper to fly by People Express Airlines than it is to rent a car or take a bus."

See what happens when you're *not* into concept-selling? The railroad companies failed to be, which contributed to their demise. They were so focused on railroads that they forgot that they were in the transportation business! They wore blinders. They should have put their money into trucks and airplanes, but instead they concentrated only on boxcars and rails. Although most customers were attracted to the advantages of shipping by truck or air, the railroads kept selling the same antiquated product they had sold for more than a century. As a result, one of America's giant industries fell to its knees.

On a personal level, though, regardless of the product, truly great salespeople sell concepts—not products. And, as important as it is to walk into a prospect's office with an idea, you should refrain from selling until you have asked him enough questions to recognize his wants and needs. Listen to what he says. If you give him the time, he will tell you.

7

Controlling the Sale

Whenever two or more people meet, one is certain to dominate or control that meeting. When that meeting is between you (the salesperson) and a prospect, *you* must be the one who maintains control throughout that meeting or you will lose the sale. That's a fact of life! In every sales interview, someone makes a sale. You either sell the prospect on the need for your product, or he sells you on why he doesn't need it. The individual who controls the sale does the selling; if you want to succeed in your sales career, you had better be that person!

When you control the sales interview, you direct the prospect's mind so he can make a buying decision in an orderly manner. You keep him on target. I always assume that the prospect wouldn't have made an appointment to see me if he weren't interested in what I have to say and the product I'm presenting. I always believe that he wants me to guide him to a buying decision that will be as painless as possible. It's your responsibility to steer the conversation and set the pace. No matter what distractions occur (phone calls, secretaries), it's your job to smoothly direct the prospect's attention back to your message. You must keep his attention! If he loses his concentration, you will probably lose the sale. When you are successfully selling eye-to-eye, you are successfully blocking out all negative interference and stimuli.

It's important to recognize that it's common behavior for many people to avoid making a buying decision. To these people, any buying decision is difficult because they don't want to risk making an error. So, rather than taking decisive action, they procrastinate. With this in mind, a prospect will frequently attempt to take the salesman's control away from him. He will try to sidetrack the sales presentation in an effort to abort the sale.

A prospect may attempt to sidetrack you in many subtle ways. He may offer you a drink or something to eat. Or he may want to show you his stamp collection or recent vacation photographs. Some salespeople think they win "extra points" by going along with these distractions. I don't. I never allow myself to be sidetracked, because I know it will cause me to lose control. I never accept any offers of food or drink, not even a glass of water. Any activity that's not directly related to my selling effort is a distraction that I must avoid. If I were asked to look at a stamp collection, I'd reply, "Let's see if we have time after we finish our business. What we are doing now is simply too important." Then I get right back into the sale.

You must remember the reason why you're there. You're there to sell. You only help the prospect when you do sell. This is the sole purpose for your visit. It's what you are compensated for. That's it, and nothing else!

How to Control the Sale

Enthusiasm is one of your most powerful allies. Your voice and body language will signal it to your prospect, and the air will be filled with inspiration! I am sure you've felt this excitement when in the company of certain individuals. This enthusiasm creates the best atmosphere for your sales presentation. It establishes a positive immediacy that puts the customer in a buying mood. *It establishes your control.*

You must keep control during the warm-up session. Many salespeople are hesitant to ask questions because they fear that the prospect, by responding, will take off on a tangent and consequently take control of the interview. But if you know how to conduct an effective warm-up session, this will not happen. When you ask pertinent questions, the other person must think about the answer; and his mind won't wander. If the prospect vacillates, say, "Now take your time and think for a moment. This is important."

The question-and-answer session is a very effective way to control the sale. What happens is that you focus the prospect's mind by *making him think about how he should answer.* I recommend that when you first start the warm-up session, you ask a difficult question that requires some thought. That will set the tone and seriousness of the interview. Ask relevant questions. Demonstrate that you're knowledgeable and *interested* in the welfare of your customer. And always project your sincerity. The more thoughtful the questions you ask, and the more interested you are in his answers, the more confidence you instill. This confidence is essential because, without it, you cannot control the sales interview. You don't want the prospect's mind to be occupied with negative thoughts such as, "Boy, is this salesman ever high pressure!" and "How am I going to get rid of this guy?" Once he's turned you off, you will lose the sale.

In a way, a salesperson and client have a relationship similar to that of a doctor and his patient or an attorney and his client. Surely you've experienced the cross-examination conducted by a doctor and an attorney during one of their warm-up sessions. That's how a sales interview can be controlled by a salesperson. It's something you must work at, however; like any other skill, you must develop it through repetition. With enough practice, you'll develop the finesse that a top-notch trial attorney uses when he cross-examines a witness. By his sequence of questions he is always focusing the witness's mind, controlling the direction of his thoughts! A good newspaper reporter knows how to ask questions, never relinquishing control to the interviewee. He, too, like the professional salesperson, jots down notes during his interview, always showing concern with each answer.

To stay in control, you must allow the prospect to participate in the sales interview. Your questions must draw him in. Most people have a short attention span, and they can't sit still and listen for long periods of time. You must bring them into the act as quickly as possible!

In some fields where a tangible product is sold, you

can get the customer to participate by having him do something physical. For example, a word-processing salesperson might have his prospect actually working away at the keyboard, moving, copying, and deleting. "Now push the Move key," the salesperson instructs the prospect, "and you'll move the third paragraph on page three to page seven, and the entire document will automatically be paginated." Salespeople selling other office machines such as computers, typewriters, and copiers, may also have their customers "doing things" that require them to think about the product, never allowing their thoughts to wander away from the sales presentation.

My best sales aid is a blank sheet of paper and a pencil. However, some salespeople use a blackboard, a flip chart, or even slides or an elaborate film presentation. These are good sales tools that can be used to keep the prospect's attention, but be careful not to overdo them. While these sales aids are supposed to make the sales presentation go more smoothly, there's a tendency for them to be complicated and dull. Try to keep things simple. Never give the prospect too many options to deal with. (No more than three, some say.) Too many choices cause confusion and invite procrastination. But if you show three models at different prices, it's believed that half the people will take the middle one, 25 percent the most expensive, and 25 percent the lowest-priced model.

Always remember that the more complicated and dragged-out a sales presentation is, the more opportunity there is to lose control of the sale. A busy person wants to soak up all the information he needs in the least amount of time. So stick to the point and don't overstay your welcome. Your client will respect that you work on a tight schedule and are a no-nonsense person. Successful people admire salespeople who get right down to business, stick to the subject, and get the job done in the least amount of time.

The length of a presentation never determines its value. For instance, I have clients who pay a thousand dollars to meet with me at my office for tax-saving consultations. Although a client may come to my Lakeland, Florida, office from as far away as the state of Washington, if it takes only an hour to give him the information he needs, that's exactly how much time he gets. When somebody asks me how much time I'll spend with him for the fee, I reply, "As long as it takes to get the job done. You can go to a barber who will cut your hair in fifteen minutes for thirty-five dollars, or another who will take an hour and charge you five dollars. What difference does it make if it's fifteen minutes or fifteen hours? The important thing is that it's the right job for you."

Did you know that some of Picasso's drawings took him only a few minutes? And they're priceless. Yet, another artist could spend months on a painting, and it wouldn't approach the value of a Picasso doodle. So the amount of time it takes to get the job done isn't really the issue, is it? The issue is getting the job done as quickly, effectively, and painlessly as possible. An individual's talent and expertise will be the determining factor.

Giving "Little Orders"

There are "little orders" good salespeople subtly give to people that play an important role in controlling a sales interview. This is something I do many times during a sales presentation, and in fact start doing even during my telephone interview while setting up an appointment. For instance, I'll say, "Fred, I would like for you to have all the necessary people there on Tuesday afternoon in order for a decision to be made." With some clients, I'll ask them to have certain documents available for me to review—perhaps their wills or financial statements.

An automobile salesperson might say, "Be sure to bring in the car that you want to trade for a new one." A stockbroker might request that his client have his portfolio available. And other salespeople may simply say, "Be sure to have your checkbook available."

One of the first things I frequently tell a prospect when I begin my sales presentation is, "Have your secretary hold all calls, but have her available so she can get certain information I might request." When I'm in a client's home and his wife is present, I'll say, "I suggest that you sit next to each other, because what I am going to tell you, I'll be showing you as well." I then sit opposite them and present my material to them right-side-up. After doing this enough, I've learned to read and write quite well *upside down!* Particularly my sales material that I'm so familiar with. I'll suggest where different people should sit at a business conference too, so everybody can view what I show.

A top commercial real-estate broker gives little orders during his sales presentation too, while selling a large shopping-center complex. "Let's walk through the mall," he says to his client, "so you can observe how nicely each retailer's windows are displayed." Later he says, "Notice the type of shopper the mall attracts. As you can see, we cater to an affluent market.

Now, I want you to sit down and notice the flow of traffic. . . ."

A salesperson selling jet airplanes to private industry might tell his client to sit in the cockpit during a demonstration. "Here, you take the wheel," he says, knowing that his customer is properly licensed. "I want you to get the feel of it." Later he advises, "Take it up to ten thousand feet." "Say, you did that very well. Now I want you to put it on instrument. . . ."

As you can see, it doesn't matter what you sell, it's easy to give little orders and get the customer into the act. The main purpose for doing this is to get the prospect into the habit of doing what you tell him. By the time you're ready to close the sale, the prospect will be conditioned to respond to such orders as, "Put your okay right here," and "Make out your check to XYZ Company."

Some Words of Caution About Controlling the Sale

Controlling the sale requires finesse. Don't be overly aggressive! Most people resent a pushy salesperson who comes across too strong. Learn to keep your voice down—it's more effective to speak in a low, soft voice. I speak very softly; and I find that the more softly I speak, the more closely people listen. People have said to me, "Joe, you're entirely different from the way I thought you'd be. You're so low-key." I like that, because I work at it.

There's a thin line between controlling the sale and being overbearing. A few years back, some best-selling books on the subject of power and the art of intimidation were popular. I resented these books that endorse the manipulation of people. One book, for example, went as far as suggesting that an executive shorten the legs on his office chairs so that his visitors would have to look up to him. The book went on to suggest that a visitor's chair should face a window with the afternoon sun glaring into his eyes. Unfortunately, many sales-people, as well as executives who read these books, were misled to believe success is attained through the use of such devious practices. I don't buy those tactics. I am successful because I believe in my product and in myself—and because I sincerely care about the people I sell to.

While it's true that people want a salesman to be assertive and show them how to buy, the salesman must always treat them with respect. In other words, use finesse. It's all right to tell people what to do, but you don't have to shove it down their throats. It's all right to let the prospect know you're an expert in your field, but don't be arrogant and talk down to him. That's not what I mean by controlling the sale, and it certainly doesn't demonstrate that you have the customer's best interests at heart.

Fortunately, the majority of people who succeed in this world do so because they do care about others. I think Somerset Maugham had the right idea when he said, "The common idea that success spoils people by making them vain, egotistical, and self-complacent is erroneous; on the contrary, it makes them, for the most part, humble, tolerant, and kind. Failure makes people bitter and cruel."

To summarize, controlling the sale is focusing a person's mind so he can make a logical buying decision. As a professional salesperson, you must control the sales interview, for your prospect's sake as well as for your own. You must conduct a detailed warm-up session in order to guide your prospect properly. He will readily recognize your expertise by the pertinent questions you ask him. Likewise, your careful listening will demonstrate your sincerity; and he'll want to do business with you.

While every salesperson must develop the skills to control the sale, a fine line exists between doing this with finesse and turning off the prospect. There are little orders that you may continually give during your presentations, but in a subtle manner without antagonizing the prospect. It's foolhardy to make him resent you! It's important for you to sell yourself, but don't become too friendly. In fact, when the prospect wants to talk about a personal interest, it becomes necessary to inform the prospect that the business at hand comes first. You're not there to make a friend but to make a sale. That's your single purpose, and that's where your full concentration must be focused. With this intensity, you will be the one who controls the sale.

8

How to Overcome
Every Objection

I've heard sales managers tell their sales forces, "Objections are merely requests for more information." I say, *Baloney!* They insist, "Each objection you diffuse brings you a step closer to closing the sale." I say, *They've got to be kidding.*

Look, the prospect who needs more information from you—to help expedite his decision to buy—will be up-front about it. He won't play games with you. Why would he *disguise* a sincere request for information? He wouldn't. But believe this: *When your would-be client starts tossing objections at you, he's sending you a message, loud and clear. He's telling you that your presentation went astray. It missed the mark. He is saying, "You might as well start packing up, because I ain't buying!"* At least, he's not buying from you—and he's not telling you why. Now it's up to you. You have to decode those objection-messages and find out what really turned him off the sale.

I never shy away from objections, and you shouldn't either. But don't be tricked into taking those objections at face value; and don't kid yourself that just because you're fielding them without a hitch, things are going your way. Until you find out what went wrong with your presentation and correct it, the objections will keep flying—and I guarantee you that they will keep on until you give up and go home.

When you review a presentation that turned sour, consider it from the beginning. You did your homework, right? If you weren't convinced that this person was a legitimate prospect, you wouldn't have expended the time, energy, and expense to make and then keep the appointment. This prospect has a need for your product and can afford it! You knew that when you began your presentation; and his flinging objections to you as fast as you can handle them doesn't change that fact. He still needs your product and he can still afford it. So, what went wrong? This may be difficult for you to accept, but chances are *the prospect doesn't trust you!* After you've banged your head against the objection-wall, answering all his concerns about price, discount, availability, color, size, delivery, service, financing, etc., etc., etc., and you still haven't reached the dotted line, you'd better start believing that this guy doesn't trust you.

Objections are usually a smoke screen that a prospect is throwing up because he can't tell you the real reason why he's resisting your presentation. In our society, few people are so straightforward as to come out and say: "I don't trust you." "You don't look me straight in the eye when you speak to me." "You don't listen to what I tell you." "You lack conviction and sincerity." "You're too aggressive." "You lack self-esteem." "You make me feel uneasy." "You seem cold, uncaring, and godless."

More often than not, these are the reasons prospects don't buy. And, of course, if you are frequently confronted with a barrage of objections, you have a serious problem to deal with.

"Well, if people don't trust me, Joe," I am asked, "what can I do about it?"

My answer to these salespeople is, "First, make sure you are straight with yourself and your God. If you're not comfortable with yourself, don't expect others to feel comfortable with you. Second, learn to zero in totally on your prospect, and give him your entire concentration. Get rid of all other thoughts that may enter your mind. Your single purpose is to sell your product to him, so shut out all distractions. Nothing short of a hydrogen bomb explosion should distract you. And, finally, throughout your entire presentation, be totally consumed with how you can best serve your prospect."

I can guarantee you that when you sell under these conditions, you will get very few objections. I am rarely faced with objections, because I practice what I preach!

Handling the Most Common Objections

Even though you know that there's much more to objections than what appears on the surface, you have to deal with them as you try to rebuild the prospect's trust. Handle the objections as calmly, pleasantly, and intelligently as you can. Don't get angry, don't panic, and don't give up. You've invested a lot of precious time already. Here's how I recommend handling the most common objections—the ones that all salespeople are bound to hear:

"You want to close this sale, but *I want to think it over.*"

"May I ask you a question? What additional information will be available later that isn't available today in order for you to make a decision?"

I wait for an answer. By letting the prospect talk, he may talk himself out of the objection. I might also add, "John, successful people usually make important decisions when all the facts are fresh in their minds. And even the most intelligent of them can't retain a hundred percent of the information they hear for even a few hours. The law of diminishing returns sets in. By the following day, they might retain seventy-five percent of what they heard. And, by the next day, they might retain only fifty percent; and so on. So, the very best time to make a decision is now. If you need more information, this is the time to get it—while you have an expert like me here to advise you."

Let him think about it, and wait for an answer. If you sense that you've softened the objection, move to the close—the credit application, contract, whatever.

"*I want to shop around,*" or "*I want to see what else is on the market.*" This is a dead giveaway that you have lost the prospect's trust—and a tough objection to field. Obviously the prospect sees a need for the product—or he wouldn't be involved in seeing what else is on the market—so there's still hope.

In the insurance field, I can broker out the business with any company, so I might say, "Hey, I'm your personal shopper. I can get commissions from everyone and can show you anything you want to see."

But the most straightforward approach here is probably the best—even though it may be risky. Look the prospect in the eye and ask, "Do you trust me? Do you think I'm representing myself and my product honestly? Because if you do, we should be able to do business now." Wait for an answer—no matter how long it takes.

"I want to see my brother-in-law (next-door neighbor, old fraternity brother, etc.) *who's in the business."*

"My clients have expressed to me that they don't want to do business with a relative or friend, John. If something goes wrong, it's awkward to have to ask your friend to service you. Besides, do you really want to share with a friend or relative the kind of confidential information necessary to implement this deal?" I'll also say, "John, you can't afford to allow friendships to be the decisive factor in such important matters. You want to make sure you and your family are getting the best consulting for your money, and I am an expert in my field."

"I can't afford it."

If you have properly screened your prospect prior to your sales interview, you know that he probably *can* afford to buy. So you have to do some prodding to find out if the information you have is correct. Of course, if he really can't afford it, offer a lower-priced alternative.

Sometimes when a prospect tells me that he can't afford it, I'll say, "May I ask you a question? Why did you allow this interview? Why did you allow me to come in here if you couldn't afford it? Now, what's the real reason?"

"I want to talk it over with my spouse."

This objection is a difficult one to overcome at the end of the sales presentation. You're better off dealing with it up front, before you begin the sales interview. Early in my career, I used to hear this objection so often that I started telling each prospect to have his wife (or her husband) present at the sales appointment. If the spouse wasn't available, I'd change our date or make darned sure that the one could make a decision without the other. If he claimed that he was the decision-maker, I'd say, "It's just great to sit down with a person who doesn't need to talk over anything with anybody and can make his own decision."

If the "unneeded" spouse is available, I always ask, "Is it necessary for him to sit in this meeting for a decision to be made? If so, I would like for him to sit in on this." However, if I'm told no, I don't want him sitting in.

Discovering the Real *Objection*

Occasionally a prospect does have a legitimate objection other than mistrust—but still hides it behind a false objection. No matter how effectively you answer it, your rebuttal won't satisfy his real objection. For example, a prospect might say to an insurance agent, "I never heard of your company, and I want to check it out." However, he simply can't afford the high premium and is embarrassed to admit it.

You can certainly diffuse his voiced concerns about

your company. Show him the company's annual report, their ratings in Dun & Bradstreet, and perhaps
several endorsement letters from satisfied customers.
But you aren't a step closer to the sale—because his
real (though unspoken) objection, a financial one, still
prevents his making a decision to buy. Unless the agent
is able to drag out the real problem, he will never convince the prospect to buy.

Another prospect's real problem might be that he
doesn't have authority to make a buying decision without his partner, or a superior, present. He's too embarrassed, however, to admit that he doesn't have the sole
authority. In the meantime, you are trying your darnedest to overcome a phony objection: "I don't feel as
though your computer can be programmed to handle
our accounts-receivable problems."

You know that it can, and you set about proving
your machine's capabilities. But you're barking up the
wrong tree, aren't you, because the real objection
hasn't been dealt with . . . the prospect's inability to
make the buying decision.

How do you tell when a prospect is expressing a
real objection? Generally, if you give a solid answer
and it doesn't seem to faze him, you should begin to
suspect that he is not leveling with you. Or, after you
have answered his objection and he throws out another, you can believe that you're getting sucked into
the old objection-trap. You just have to do some fish-
ing until you're satisfied. Ask more questions. Listen
very carefully. (You might have failed to listen during
your warm-up session.) As a last resort, I sometimes
say, "I know your objections—those you've shared
with me—but I feel that there's more to it. What is the

real reason?" Then, if he doesn't volunteer an answer, I'll add, "You do trust me, don't you?"

Sidestepping Objections

Sometimes when a prospect gives me an objection for the first time, I ignore it and continue with my close. For example, a prospect might say, "I ought to take some time to think it over." Instead of picking up on it, I assume the sale by muttering, "I understand. How much do you weigh and how tall are you?"

I'll go right through the health application, and in many cases the prospect will never repeat that he wanted to think it over.

Another might say, "Joe, I never do business with a stranger on the first call. I want to sleep on it."

"Me either, but we stopped being strangers as soon as I walked through that door." And then I go on as though he agreed.

Bringing It Down to One Last Objection

"Your only objection for not wanting this policy is due to worry over paying the premiums in the event you become disabled?"

"That's right, Joe."

"But if there were some way that you didn't have to pay them when you were disabled, you'd want the policy? Gosh, that's a good reason, and I see what you mean. Now that's the only reason, right?"

"Right."

Now I've backed him into a corner. If I overcome this one objection, I will get the sale. Of course, for this objection I explain that a waiver-of-premium clause could be put on the policy for only a few dollars more; and it will do exactly what he wants—it will pay the premium during a period of total disability.

A salesperson selling a word processor might say, "Now, let me get this straight. Your only objection is that this word processor can't handle your accounts-receivable as a computer does. But if it could, it would do everything you need and you'd want it." Once the prospect agrees that it's the only reason, the salesperson explains how certain software could be programmed so the machine could handle his accounts receivable. Again the prospect is backed into a corner—because he just admitted this was his only reason for not buying the word processor.

In each of the above instances, the salesperson didn't have to wait for the prospect's acknowledgment that the objection was overcome and that he would now buy. The salesperson automatically assumed the sale.

To recap what I stated at the beginning of this chapter, the majority of objections are given because the prospect doesn't trust you. In these instances, no matter how well you handle his objections, unless you do something to rebuild his lost confidence in you, you're not going to get the sale. Although you're at the end of the sales presentation and still getting objections and your back may be against the wall, it doesn't necessarily mean the sale is lost.

Handling the Procrastinator

Some people have a difficult time making decisions about things that are out of their field of expertise. This is true even with people who make big decisions every day in their own businesses. For example, I have had surgeons who couldn't decide on a life insurance policy; yet these same individuals make split-second life-and-death decisions in the operation room doing open-heart surgery. I have seen the same thing with real-estate developers who make multimillion-dollar on-the-spot decisions. However, when taken away from their field of expertise, they have difficulty in reaching a buying decision. Sometimes they agonize over the items on a menu.

If given the opportunity, these people will procrastinate or vacillate because they are afraid of making a wrong decision. It's as simple as that. In these cases, the mental gymnastics are: "If I don't spend my money, I'm in the same position as before I heard the sales presentation. However, if I do spend my money, there's a chance I might spend it unwisely."

It's your job as a salesperson to convince these people that the wrong decision is to do nothing. People like this remind me of Buridan's Ass. That's the fable where the ass starved himself to death standing between two stacks of hay because he was unable to decide which was the more desirable.

I think these people sincerely want to buy, but they are relying on you to be more persuasive so they can take decisive action *now*. When they say, "I want to think it over," they're really telling you, "If you can convince me today, I will buy today." I don't think these people want to be indecisive, and you're relieving them of considerable discomfort by guiding them with their decision-making.

One way I handle the prospect who can't make up his mind is by saying, "Dick, one way or another a decision will be made now, even though you think it might be best to make no decision. You may decide that this investment of a five-thousand-dollar premium is wrong because it could prove to be unnecessary at some later point. In a sense, if that happened, it could even be regarded as a five-thousand-dollar mistake. While none of us likes to make even a one-dollar mistake, your life-style will not be altered in any way by that sort of minor mistake. So by deferring this decision today and doing nothing, you will have made a decision. And in your mind you will have saved spending five thousand dollars. But that could turn out to be a five-hundred-thousand-dollar mistake, especially if you become uninsurable or die prematurely. Now, both of us know what's best for your family, Dick. Let's go ahead and submit this application and set up a date for your physical examination."

A salesperson selling a word processor to a law firm might say something similar. "Ted, I know that fifteen thousand dollars sounds like a lot of money to invest in office equipment at this time. But all the major law firms in town are investing in this equipment today; and if you don't have one, your firm is going to have a difficult time giving quick service to your clients. Besides, while fifteen thousand is a large expense, you can pay for it over a five-year lease buy-back; and when you consider the money you'll save in secretarial time, you'll end up being many dollars ahead. This word processor won't cost you money—it will save you money." After a slight pause, the salesperson assumes the close by adding, "Now sign your name on the dotted line. And press hard—there are four copies."

By the way, have you noticed how the sale is assumed in all of the examples I use in this book? I'll cover assuming the sale in detail in Chapter 9, but for now I want to point out how taking this positive action is so important in handling objections. When a salesperson exudes self-esteem, and confidently asks for the order, the prospect will have a tendency to respond positively. On the other hand, if a salesperson gets shaken up when objections are thrown at him, the prospect's doubts are reconfirmed that he should not make a buying decision. Just as enthusiasm and confidence are contagious, so is hesitation!

When a procrastinator is having a painful time making a decision, he needs reinforcement from the salesperson. The last thing he needs is a Mr. Milquetoast who hems and haws his replies to the procrastinator. It's what I call the monkey-see, monkey-do principle. So you must be sure that your prospect perceives you as a strong, intelligent decision-maker. Generate decisiveness!

Did you ever walk into an automobile dealership with every intention of buying a car that afternoon? However, for some reason you walked out without making a purchase, feeling dejected. For some reason—you can't put your finger on it—you didn't buy a car. You liked the product, and didn't dislike the salesperson!

When you think back and analyze what happened, it's likely that you encountered an indecisive salesperson. *He generated indecisiveness.* On the other hand, recall the times when you have walked into a showroom only to look around. But, before you knew it, you walked out having purchased an automobile, a suit, or perhaps a new stereo. And you really felt good about it. Most likely, you encountered a highly positive, self-confident salesperson—and he generated positive vibrations that made you react decisively. Again, you mimicked his positive qualities. He made you feel confident that you could make a major buying decision that day—so you did!

Again, the monkey-see, monkey-do principle applies. The prospect knows the salesperson is decisive, so he isn't about to appear meek and unable to make up his mind. This is the reaction I get from the macho-type man when I say, "You know, it's a real pleasure to meet somebody like you who can make up his mind without his wife's permission. There are so many guys around nowadays who always have to run to their wives for their permission. I admire decisiveness like yours!" Hearing this, the prospect doesn't want to disappoint me by showing that he can't make up his mind—he doesn't want to appear to be a weakling! On the other hand, a prospect feels no shame in displaying his own weakness to a salesperson whom he perceives to be weak.

Once again, objections are most apt to occur when something goes wrong in the sales presentation. Ideally, with a perfect presentation, objections are nonexistent. But perfect presentations are not always given; and to complicate matters, prospects are likely to voice false objections rather than expressing their real reasons for not buying. How do you go about avoiding these situations? Make sure your entire act is together. Speak with sincerity, conviction, and enthusiasm. Be prepared to deal with common objections that are bound to occur. Anticipate that it's natural for some prospects to procrastinate—especially if you let them. Your job is to make buying your product an easy decision. *Be trustworthy.* Project that trust and make the sale.

9

Closing the Sale

I hesitate even to write a chapter on closing the sale, because it's no big deal. Yet, this is the single most asked-about subject when I field questions at sales seminars. Many salespeople are confident about their ability to sell but too often find themselves stifled at the very moment the sale should be in their pocket—the close. Hence, they want to know how to overcome what they believe is their major stumbling block.

Believe me when I tell you that if you do everything right from your first approach and throughout your presentation, *closing the sale is automatic*. In this sense, the close is *the moment of truth*. It's your reward for a job well done. I don't give much thought to closing the sale because I work my tail off making sure that everything falls into place—knowing the sale will follow as surely as day follows night.

Unfortunately, most salespeople don't do enough right, enough of the time. And until they get their acts together, they're going to need all the help available—

especially in the area where they will get the most resistance. So, for those of you who fall into this category,
I am including a chapter on closing the sale. In the
meantime, however, I suggest that you practice what
I've told you in Chapters 1 through 8, because, the
better you are in the early stages of your sales presentation, the less you'll have to be concerned about the
closing.

Nothing Happens Until Something Is Sold!

Let's get one thing straight: you don't make sales
presentations for the sake of entertaining people or in-
forming them. The only value of an aborted sales presentation is the experience you got out of it—if you're
smart enough to learn from your mistakes!

Your job is to *help* the prospect, and the best way to
accomplish this is by helping him buy your product. If
you sincerely believe in its value, you must convince
him that the benefit of having your product outweighs
the price he must pay to obtain it. Only when you are
successful are you doing him a fine service.

Forget about how you will benefit when he buys
your product. Be *consumer-oriented.* Sure, I know you
may have a family to feed and a roof to put over their
heads. So what else is new? Your prospect isn't going
to give you an order just because you need the money.
That's no reason for him to buy! He has to be the party
who benefits, not you. And if he does, your money will
eventually come, I promise you. Forget that the prospect represents income to you. Like the song says,
"Don't count your money till the playing is done."
Your job is to help the prospect, and in order to do

that, you must place his interests above yours. In fact, you should be so consumer-oriented that you should refuse to sell to a prospect who can't afford your product or who for some other reason would be better off without it. You may pass up a few easy sales, but if you're a salesperson who thinks only in terms of helping others, you will have a prosperous career.

A salesperson should not have the attitude that he is matching his wits against the prospect's. It is wrong to create the kind of competitive atmosphere in which one party wins and the other loses. Instead, you must assume the position of being on the same team. Again, I bring to your attention the relationship that exists between doctor/patient and attorney/client. The same must be present with a salesperson/customer. You must establish a feeling of teamwork, not opposition.

The Fear of Rejection

Many salespeople are weak at closing sales because they fear rejection. Once into a sales presentation, these individuals often reach a "comfort level" that they don't want to shatter. To them, the close is perceived as a confrontation that will destroy the pleasant relationship they have achieved. Generally, these salespeople are the same ones who have difficulty with their approach.

In time, practically everyone learns how to explain his product effectively. Even the weakest salesperson has little difficulty in explaining the nuts and bolts about his product. So it's smooth sailing until the close. Thus far, it's been rather cozy, and he enjoys the friendly relationship established with the prospect.

However, sooner or later the moment of truth is bound to occur. And the meek salesperson will be afraid to ask for the order because *he might get rejected*. Instead, he talks and talks, and he talks himself right out of the sale.

So he didn't make the sale—and he didn't help the prospect—and he didn't make a friend. In the long run, you can build a friendship only if you close the sale.

Closing with Conviction and Confidence

Throughout this book, I have stressed selling with conviction and confidence. These are absolutely necessary ingredients in every part of your sales presentation. Needless to say, you can't abandon these qualities at the close.

You must have full confidence in your ability to close the sale. Because if you don't, the prospect will begin to wonder about you—and he will become consumed with doubt. He *knows* when your presentation is over. He expects you to ask for the sale. Let's face it: he knew that you were a salesperson when he agreed to see you. Remember my monkey-see, monkey-do analogy: if you lack confidence in closing the sale, the prospect will lack confidence in making a decision.

Some salespeople tell me, "Joe, if I were successful like you, I'd have the confidence." I tell these people that it's the old question about which came first, the chicken or the egg. As you gain little successes, your confidence level keeps increasing; and eventually, by seeing enough people, you start to believe in yourself.

It's a fact that successful people have self-confidence. When you close the sale with confidence, you personify success; and as the old adage goes, *success breeds success.* We all like to deal with successful people. We think to ourselves, "There's a reason why this salesman is successful. He's good, and so his company and his product must be good."

Creating a Sense of Urgency

One way to build a fire under the seat of a procrastinating prospect is to create a sense of urgency. It doesn't matter what you sell—if you think it through, you can find an urgency.

In the life insurance business, it's very easy. A prospect's health may change so that he becomes uninsurable. A delay on his part may mean that tomorrow or next week he won't be able to qualify. "Jack, none of us has a crystal ball and can see into the future. Heaven forbid you should die before you qualify for this policy. Your family would be destitute. Let's pray that you can qualify as quickly as possible." A "tomorrow is too late" consciousness is created. And rates increase as one's age changes.

A real-estate agent creates a sense of urgency when he says, "Let me tell you something, Bruce and Nancy. I know you want to think it over, but at this reduced price, this house may be gone before the day is over. Another agent is showing it this afternoon, and I have two more showings tomorrow. I suggest that we submit an offer as soon as we get back to my office." With a one-of-a-kind product such as a real-estate property, a true sense of urgency can be presented.

A computer salesperson creates a sense of urgency

in perhaps a different way. He can't tell his prospect that if he doesn't act now the product might not be available. So, instead, he sells the pressing need of having a computer installed as quickly as possible so the prospect can begin having his business run more efficiently. "Jon, the longer you wait to put it in, the more critical your inventory problem becomes. As you said, your shipping department is already six weeks behind schedule. How long can you continue to do business like that? In your own words, and I'll quote you, your present system is 'creating a Frankenstein's monster.' May I use your phone to call my office to see if we can have a computer installed this week?"

It's easy for a stockbroker to create a sense of urgency in selling a particular stock—as it is if you're selling any product or commodity that shows frequent price changes. The "limited offer" was designed to create a sense of urgency; the prospect must act quickly in order to take advantage of it. In a somewhat primitive way, we see such offers every day on television and at the supermarket: "Send in just $11.95 today and receive not one record album, not two, but three." "Send in $19.95 today and we will ship you all fifteen pots and pans. But act now while our supply lasts." "Today's special, only one to a customer. . . ." "Special, only 99¢."

While these limited-offer examples are not exactly sophisticated, the same technique works with expensive products. For example, a word-processing salesperson might tell his prospect, "The company will be having a major price increase on the first of the month. Now, that's only two days away, so I suggest we put your order in today." A copier salesperson might inform his customer that the company is having a special on copying paper which expires by the end of the week. A real-estate agent may inform his client that if he waits, he'll be liable for the real-estate taxes due on the property. As you can see, there are many limited-offer techniques that create a sense of urgency and urge the prospect to *act today*.

The Minor-Major Close

While a procrastinator has a difficult time making major decisions, it's not hard for him to make minor ones. With this in mind, the minor-major close presents many minor decisions for the prospect to make—all adding up to a major one.

A good car salesperson would be likely to use this closing technique when selling a car to an old customer who, he knows from previous experience, has difficulty making a decision. An example of offering him a major decision would be, "Just $15,750 and this baby is yours, Mr. Williams. What do you say?"

That's a very difficult decision for Mr. Williams to make. He will probably need some time to mull it over.

However, by using the minor-major close, the salesman would give Mr. Williams a series of minor decisions to make—little ones such as, "Do you like the two-door or the four-door?"

"Oh, I think I'll go for the two-door."

"Which of these three colors do you like, Mr. Williams?"

"I like the yellow."

"Do you want AM or FM radio?"

"AM is fine."

"Do you want it undercoated?"

"Absolutely."

"Tinted glass?"

"It's not necessary."

"Whitewall tires?"

"No, thanks."

"We can deliver it on October first or on the eighth."

"The first would be better."

After asking many minor questions that are easy for his customer to decide upon, the salesperson hands the order pad to him and says matter-of-factly, "Okay this line, Mr. Williams, so your order can be processed."

Since each of the earlier decisions were easy for him to make, he has no problem signing his name acknowledging all of them. And by doing so, he gives his consent to put in the order.

In the insurance industry, a minor-major close is also used. Again, the consent to make a major decision is avoided. For example, the agent doesn't say, "If you want this million-dollar policy, I'll need a check for $14,220." Instead, he too asks minor questions:

"Should we put down your wife as the beneficiary?"

"Yes."

"Do you want to pay for it annually, semiannually, or quarterly?"

"Semiannually."

"Do you want the waiver of premium?"

"No."

"How about accidental death?"

"No."

"Okay this application on this line, please."

See how easy it is when you give them minor decisions rather than major ones? The minor-major close is designed to take the pain out of making a major decision for the person who can't make up his mind.

Assuming the Sale

"Hey, Joe," I am often asked, "when do you begin to assume the sale?" My answer is that I assume the sale as soon as I set up the appointment for the sales interview. I figure that any person interested in seeing me has a need for my product. If not, he wouldn't schedule the appointment in the first place. So I assume the sale immediately. I walk into his office with this attitude, and it prevails throughout the sales interview. In fact, everything I do is geared to the assumption that the prospect is going to buy. I believe this thinking has a very positive influence on the prospect's decision-making.

Now that you know *when* I begin to assume the sale, let me run by some specific ways that you can assume the sale as a closing technique. When I begin asking questions on the life insurance application, the client knows that I expect him to buy now! I automatically ask, "Jim, how tall are you and how much do you weigh?" We both know we're in the homestretch now.

The alternative to assuming the sale is to ask for it directly. "Jim, may I ask you some questions on this application?" If I did that, he'd have an opportunity to respond, "Well, I think I'd like to sleep on this for a couple of nights." He knows that the application is the moment of truth, the big decision—and I'm dumping it all into his lap. That's a tough decision for him to make, But when I assume the sale by going right into the question session with him, it's easy for him to consent to answering the questions—because there's no decision-making required.

Assuming the sale is one of the most basic closes. It's done in a subtle way that doesn't offend anyone. For example, years ago Gulf Oil trained their gasoline attendants to assume the sale when they approached a customer by asking, "Shall I fill it up with No-Nox, sir?" Two things are assumed by this question: first, that you want the maximum amount of gasoline your tank can hold; second, that you want the most expensive kind of gasoline that Gulf sells. If they simply asked the customer, "What kind of gas do you want and how much?" you can imagine how much easier it would be for the decision to be, "Oh, give me five dollars' worth of regular."

Observe how many times you hear today, "Would you like to charge it to your Visa, MasterCard, or American Express?" The airline, car-rental, and hotel industries use this closing technique when you call for information regarding reservations. Most retailers also assume the sale by asking for your credit card. I have always assumed that my prospect would buy by asking, "Do you want to pay by check or cash?" Again, it's not a question of whether you want to pay. Today, when I sell large policies with premiums of five figures and up, it would be unreasonable to ask for cash. So, now I assume the sale by saying, "Make out your check for $12,500 to the company, not to me personally." Again, I didn't ask the question, "Do you want to buy this policy? If so, it costs $12,500."

A salesperson can ask a whole host of questions, and

if one of them doesn't close the sale, another can be tried. In fact, it's common to make several attempts to assume the sale during a presentation. Here are a few common ones:

> "Do you want to handle it monthly or quarterly?"
> "Which of these two premiums would best fit your present financial situation?"
> "Do you want the $5 million or $10 million policy?" (When you're selling big-ticket items such as I do, you might want to qualify the question by saying, "You can always start with the biggest; and if it seems like too much, you can reduce it later on. It's harder to increase it, so let's go for as much as we can get for you now.")
> "Do you want this car with or without air conditioning?"
> "Do you want the red one or the blue one?"
> "Do you want cuffs put on your pants, or do you want them without cuffs?"

Being sold a suit by a good clothing salesman is a fine example of how to assume the sale, an example that we've all seen. After you try on the suit to see how it fits, the salesman doesn't ask if you want it. Instead, he leads you over to the mirror and has you look at yourself in it. "Say, you look great!" he says, pulling the jacket in a little and adding, "We'll have to take some in right here."

He calls to his tailor—still holding the back of the suit jacket—and asks, "How does it look to you?"

"We'll have to take it in right here and here," the tailor says. Studying the fit, he draws chalk marks on the suit.

"How about the waist?" the salesman asks.

"Let's see how it fits," the tailor says. As he tightens up the waistline, he comments, "We'll take it in here, and the seat needs to be let out a little right here." He pauses and says, "Sir, is this about where you wear your pants?"

"Er, yeah, that's right," the customer replies.

Again the tailor uses his chalk, this time to mark the length of the trousers. "Do you like cuffs, sir?"

"No."

"How long will it take for the suit to be ready?" the salesman asks the tailor.

"We'll have it ready for you on Thursday," the tailor says directly to the customer.

"You look just great," the salesman comments, nodding his head approvingly.

"Come with me to the tie department and I'll help you pick out a tie to go with it," he says, leading him by the arm.

In the above example, the salesperson *and* the tailor (who obviously have worked together, teaming up on customers many times before) assume the sale again and again. Notice that they do it not just by what they say, but by their actions as well. For instance, the salesperson didn't ask the customer if he wanted to look in the mirror. He led him to the mirror by the arm. He didn't ask the customer if he was interested in buying the suit. Instead, he assumed it and immediately started tugging in the jacket to make it fit properly. The tailor then got into the act and started to chalk up the suit. After chalk was put on the jacket and the customer didn't protest that he didn't want to buy, it would have been very awkward for him to later say,

"Hey, what's going on here? I don't want this suit."

The salesperson knew the sale was in the bag when the customer gave his implied consent by *not saying no*.

Notice how the salesperson didn't stop assuming the sale upon reaching the point where he knew it was made. Instead, he kept right on going—all the way to when the customer walked out of his store. He never stopped selling: "Don't forget to ask for me when you come back again." Again, he was *assuming* the customer would come back.

As you will note, whether you're applying the minor-major closing technique or the assuming-the-sale technique, the question never is "Do you want the product?" The question is "How, when, and where do you want it?"

Buying Signals

I won't dwell on the subject, but *if you listen*, you'll pick up certain buying signals that telegraph you the prospect wants to buy your product. These signals are flashed in actions as well as words. If you observe them carefully, they will let you know when to close the sale.

The customer will ask certain questions that signal he's interested in buying your product. In the life insurance business, some of the obvious ones are: "Can I pay for it quarterly?" "How many physical examinations do I need to take?" "What does it cost the second and third year?" "Are the proceeds tax-free that are paid to my estate?"

In other fields, buying signals might be: "What would the monthly payments be?" "If I bring it in for

service, will you give me a loaner?" "When do they
deliver?" "Is there a charge for delivery?" "How does
the warranty work?" "What colors does it come in?"
"Does it come in pink?" "May I try it on?" There's an
endless list of questions that a prospect might ask;
you've got to listen to them.

You should also observe cetain physical actions. For
example, when a customer is looking in a mirror, a
clothing salesperson should study both facial expressions and body language. Another customer who takes
a particular sweater off the shelf and holds it to her
face in front of a mirror is also telling something to the
observant salesclerk. The customer who keeps playing
with the computer while the salesperson is making a
demonstration is signaling something, too. The customer who keeps walking back to the same automobile
in the showroom and sitting behind the wheel is sending out signals. There are countless buying signals to
watch for as well as to listen for.

Being a Percentage Player

Sooner or later every salesperson must learn what I
believe to be an absolute dictum about closing a sale:
You've got to be a percentage player. You will always
have prospects who say, "I want to think it over. How
about coming back in a few days?" When that's asked
of me, I say, "I'm sorry, but I can't." They may appear
to be very sincere in making this request, but my answer is always the same. So, obviously, I am convinced
that you're making a horrendous mistake if you agree
to call on these prospects again in lieu of making every
attempt to close the sale at the time of your presenta-

tion. As I stated previously, the law of diminishing returns comes into play. The longer the time between an individual's hearing a sales presentation and his making a buying decision, the lower the odds that the sale will be made. In short, the prospect simply *cools off!* His memory won't retain the reasons for buying. The time to make a decision is when all of the facts are fresh at hand—and that time is *now*.

Novice salespeople are frequently lured into the trap of making callbacks on prospects who might have been sold if the salesperson had had the tenacity to stay in there. Instead, they opt to comply with the prospect's request, only to be bitterly disappointed later. For example, one novice life insurance agent told me last November, "I'm going to have the biggest month ever in January. If only half of the prospects who promised to buy come through, I'll set a company sales record." Sadly, January was not a record-breaking month for him. He made some "fresh" sales, but wasted a lot of presentations on prospects who had promised to "buy later."

"All those promises for January cooled off and went by the wayside, Joe." I knew they would.

I told him that he should have been more persistent—insisting that the present was the time to buy, not the first of the year. In fact, in some cases there were actual tax advantages available because certain business premiums were deductible and would have been better used before year's-end. I also asked him, "How would you have felt if one of them had become uninsurable in the meantime—or, worse, had died?" I then told him that he must drum into his prospects' heads the words of Peter F. Drucker: "Long-range planning does not deal with future needs, but with the future of present decisions."

In my early days I used to experiment with prospects who seemed both sincere and determined to have me call back at a later date for their decision. I kept accurate records of the number of sales I made when I called back, and my batting average was so low that it wasn't worth my time to call back on any prospect. Later, I would even say, "I'll tell you what, John. If you are sincere, let's fill out all the papers, sign them, and you give me a postdated check; and tomorrow you can give me your decision one way or the other." Although every prospect who agreed to do that would assure me of his sincerity, the percentage that would come through was practically nil. At the time they probably were sincere—they just cooled off, that's all. It began to dawn on me that if I didn't close the sale the first time around, I wasn't going to close it later.

Callbacks just aren't worth a tinker's damn, and sooner or later you must realize this as a fact of life in selling! I'm a percentage player, so I know it's not good business to go after a 1-to-6 long shot—not when the odds are 2 to 1 that I'll close the sale if I'm tenacious enough to go for it "now or never," *today.* I'm in this business for the long run; and over a period of time, the theory of ratios always works. I guarantee that you'll be many dollars ahead if you give it your best shot—one time—and go to your next appointment.

Pressure Selling—A Very Fine Line

It's a salesperson's job to overcome procrastination and to convince the prospect that *now* is the time to make a buying decision. A salesperson who is truly good at closing will do so—and the client will thank him for it. But if the close is not handled with finesse, accusations are likely to be made that high-pressure selling tactics were used. If this happens, not only will you lose the sale, but you're probably going to infuriate the prospect.

A thin line exists between using pressure tactics and closing a sale with finesse. In both instances, you use the same selling techniques, such as the minor-major close and assuming the sale. And, similarly, you play the percentages with a "now or never" philosophy. The problem many salespeople encounter is that some prospects don't want to make up their minds—they resist being pressured to buy now. It may come to the point where a salesperson will either close the sale or, at the other extreme, push the prospect so much that he will get thrown out on his ear. For obvious reasons, you don't want to antagonize anyone to this extreme!

For the most part, this is where experience plays a big role. After a while, you get a "feel" for just how much pressure you can exert on certain prospects and not lean on them too heavily for the buying decision.

Now, I want to make this clear: *I don't* advocate pressure selling—unless it works! In other words, you've got to be good at it if you're going to do it. And I'll make no bones about it, every salesperson worth his salt must use it now and then to get those procrastinators straddling the fence to make a buying decision. But you have to be good at it, because—if you're not—it will backfire.

The salespeople most likely to be accused of pressure tactics are the ones who come across too strong.

They're glib, talk in a loud voice and much too quickly.
Above all, they seldom ask questions or listen. The
prospect has the impression that they don't really have
his interests in mind. They have dollar signs in their
eyes, and the prospect knows it! Their mannerisms signal this message to the prospect and, accordingly, he
resists them. On the other hand, those salespeople who
speak softly, listen carefully, look the prospect squarely
in the eye, project conviction, and demonstrate sincerity, don't come across as using pressure tactics. They
put the prospect at ease. He feels comfortable and has
confidence in them. Yet, these salespeople may use the
same closing techniques as those who are accused of
high-pressuring. The difference is, *they're good at using
pressure!*

So, when I'm asked if I ever use pressure, my stock
answer is, "Yes, I do, like every other top producer."
But it's done in a subtle way that doesn't turn off the
prospect. And, again, I'm a percentage player. I'm well
aware that now and then I may lose a sale because a
prospect thinks he's being high-pressured. But I can't
afford to worry about it. The prospects I sell are the
people I am most concerned about. I know that I enjoy
outstanding relationships with my clients; and in the
long run, that's what is most important.

Well, I ended up talking more about the subject of
closing the sale than I had anticipated—but I am stick-
ing to my guns that it's no big deal. If you do everything right, the close should be automatic.

Never forget that your prime reason for calling on a
prospect is to help him, and nothing happens until
something is sold. When you close the sale, you've got
to do it with conviction and confidence. You can't fear

rejection—you must anticipate the sale. If you hem and haw, so will your prospect. He will mimic your indecisiveness as well as your confidence. Just how he perceives you is how he will react—either indecisively or decisively.

With people who tend to procrastinate, it's your job to create a sense of urgency so they will make a buying decision *now*. You must instill the idea that, one way or another, a decision must be made. And to do nothing is the worst possible decision. As Edward Young said, "Procrastination is the thief of time." Get people to act now. "Don't stand shivering upon the bank; plunge in at once and have it over." Thomas Haliburton said that, and it is the message that every salesperson must get through to his prospects.

As a salesperson, it's your job to guide the prospect and make it easy for him to buy your product. One way to do this is by letting him make a major decision by making many minor ones. You must also assume the sale. You begin to do this immediately upon making your first contact with the prospect. There should never be any question as to whether he will buy—it's only a matter of how much he will buy. If you observe your prospect carefully, you will recognize certain buying signals that will let you know.

Last, when it's time to close the sale, *do it!* Play the percentages; don't buck them! It's just good business to work the odds when they're in your favor. And don't back off from exerting a little pressure when necessary. In its place, pressure selling isn't such a bad thing, and it's all part of closing the sale. All top producers use it—and with finesse, it gets the job done.

10

Good Service Is Good Selling

You worked hard to make the sale. You earned your commission and you feel good about it. You should. You converted a prospect into *your* customer. Now what?

Well, if you're like a lot of salespeople who work their fannies off and never seem to make it, you'll probably take the money and run. Oh, you might pay your new customer a little lip service, like "Look me up if you have any problems"; then forget his name before his check clears the bank. Lots of salespeople do it that way; usually they are waiting for their big break, wondering why they aren't as lucky as the big money-makers.

What the losers don't realize is that big money-makers aren't lucky, and they don't wait for breaks, and they know how to take care of a new client. To emulate the super-salesperson, you must give your new customer a lot of thought. You must make darned sure that he's glad that he met you and that he continues feeling that way. You must see to it that he never forgets your name and that you won't forget his. You must make sure that your new client becomes a customer who will buy from you again and again and again, and will recommend you to his friends and associates. There's only one way to make all this happen: You must do what I do. *Do it with service!*

Shortsighted people think that servicing is a costly waste of time—like playing a game after you've won it. They're not only shortsighted, they're foolish. Look, you have to believe that each new client is a potential gold mine; that the initial sale, no matter how exciting, is just the beginning. Each customer, properly nurtured by you, can become the base for a whole new customer list. It can build geometrically. You have to earn referrals—they don't come to you as gifts. But the payoff can be tremendous. Top salespeople depend on it. *They expect 80 percent of their sales income from referrals and repeat business!* And they achieve this by a customer service program that is well thought out and carefully implemented.

Once you commit yourself to truly servicing your customers, you become part of a wonderful minority group that has a decided advantage over the competition.

Let's face it, service is the single ingredient that separates one company from another; one salesperson from another; one product from another. In our highly competitive free-enterprise system, there's no such thing as a product so superior to its competition that outstanding service cannot make a difference. In my industry, four hundred thousand life insurance agents are all selling basically the same merchandise. And how much difference is there between a Ford and a Chevrolet?

With multiple listings in the real-estate industry, every agent in town sells the same property. In the stockbrokerage business, all licensed representatives can sell the same listed securities. In all these fields, there are salespeople who make a fortune, many more who just make a living, and plenty of losers. By now, you're getting the idea as to what it takes to break away from the pack. If you do everything that I've suggested in the first nine chapters of this book, I guarantee that you'll be more successful than most of your colleagues; but if you want to rise to the very top of your field, you must pay very close attention to the contents of this chapter and incorporate servicing into your sales philosophy and procedures as I suggest in these pages.

Communicate with Your Customer

Throughout your sales presentation you have stressed to your customer that you will give him service. With this in mind, it's a good idea to start off by dropping him a note or giving him a call after the sale letting him know how much you appreciate his business. You'd be surprised how much a brand-new customer appreciates a phone call saying, "Tom, I just called to thank you for your order yesterday. I really appreciate having an opportunity to do business with you. If there's absolutely anything I can do for you, please give me a call."

I always make it a point to send a handwritten note such as:

Dear John;

Tonight does not seem too soon to congratulate you on this afternoon's decision about your new life policy. This is certainly a major step in establishing a sound future financial program. I hope that our meeting was the beginning of a long and enduring relationship. Thank you again for your business and I wish you every success possible.

Sincerely,
Joe Gandolfo

Stop and think about it. When was the last time you received a thank-you letter when you bought a car? A copy machine? Or a fur coat? If you ever received one (I have), I bet you thought to yourself, "Say, this guy is really different from other salespeople. I feel very good about doing business with him."

The average buyer is full of built-in suspicions. Every one of us has heard the remark about salespeople: "They're always here to sell you, but where are they when you need them?" Of course, the "when you need them" refers to getting service when something goes wrong. So, your first note tips him off that he's not dealing with an ordinary salesperson. Just when he might have a slight case of "buyer's remorse," you make him think, "I was right about him after all."

Without communicating with your customer, it's impossible to give good service. Sometimes, just the fact that you communicate with him gives him peace of mind that you're doing the job he expects you to do. For example, a real-estate agent should keep in close touch with a client whose home he is trying to sell. Quite often, the agent might be doing a lot of work for his client—but the client doesn't know it. Then, when it comes to paying a 6-percent commission on a $200,000 sale, the client is upset about shelling out $12,000. The problem is that he never knew what the agent did behind the scenes because *the agent didn't tell him!*

It's too bad when the home owner has to call his real-estate agent and ask what's happening. It should be the agent who is constantly on the phone letting his client know what's going on: "Good news. First Savings and Loan has agreed to make a mortgage commitment on your home." "Two different families looked at your home today while you were at work. I'm bringing over another tomorrow at two." "A VA appraiser is coming out on Friday around five." "I'm having a photographer come to take a picture of your house for multiple-listing purposes." "I wrote this ad for you today. Let me read it back to you for your thoughts on it."

So, if you are doing things for your customer, don't keep it a secret—let him know. If you don't, you'll end up with a frustrated customer!

It's easy to report good news to your customers, but when there's some bad news, you've got to be prompt to tell them about that, too. This kind of follow-up is all part of good service, and you must act on it without delay. For instance, an insurance agent might delay contacting an applicant to tell him the disappointing news that the insurer is going to rate the policy by ten dollars per thousand. Another unpleasant call might be to tell an applicant that due to questionable health, he must take a glucose tolerance test—a four-hour blood-testing procedure! Or he might be hesitant to let his client know that the company will issue a policy for only 75 percent of the amount applied for. Even worse, he might have to call a client to inform him that the company has turned the application down. These are a few instances where insurance agents must face the music now and then—and the longer they procrastinate in relaying the news, the more difficult it is.

Every salesperson has his share of bad-news calls to make. My advice is to do them as they come in. Don't put them off and let them accumulate. A real-estate agent might have to call a home owner and tell him, "Fred, the bank just turned down the buyer's credit application." The real-estate agent might also have to let a home owner know that potential customers have complained about chipped paint, worn-out carpeting, and other needed repairs. So a call might be, "If you want to sell your home at the price you want, Fred, it's going to take some money to get it in order."

Another call that a stockbroker might make is, "Mary, I just read a very negative report on ABC Company. Now, I know you bought five thousand shares on my recommendation last week at twenty-six, but the stock dropped three points this morning and I have a fear it might drop to below twenty. I suggest we bite the bullet and sell it immediately."

An automobile salesperson should call his customer immediately when he gets disappointing news: "Stan, I just got word from Detroit that there's going to be a twelve-day delay on your car."

In these cases and others like them, you're far better off passing the bad news along as quickly as possible. When you delay, matters only get worse. Learn to accept that problems don't go away by ignoring them. If you ignore them, your customers might go away!

Bear in mind that your job is to *inform* your customers continually. You cannot overinform!

Never forget that the shortest distance between two points is *the telephone.* There's never any excuse for a salesperson not to keep in constant touch with his customers—not so long as there's a telephone service in this country!

I take pride in telling my clients that I'm on call twenty-four hours a day, weekends included. I told them that when I set up an appointment to sell them, and I've got to give them the same accessibility when they need me for servicing. You've got to be there at their convenience, not yours. It's like operating a restaurant, a service station, or a movie theater. You must work the hours that are best for your customers.

Salespeople sometimes ask me, "Joe, as your business gets bigger and bigger, is there a point at which you spend so much time servicing your existing accounts that your annual sales production begins to drop?" That's a good question, and early in my career it was one I used to ponder. Actually, through my own experience I have discovered that the exact opposite is true—*if* you build up a support system along the way (which, fortunately, I did). Bear in mind that, as you get bigger, you can afford to hire top people and purchase better equipment. As you grow, so does the capacity of your organization; and a lot of the service work that I used to do when I was new in the business is now delegated.

You can never rest on past laurels. It's also important to realize that you can't allow yourself to get too big for your britches. The bigger you get, the more you must concern yourself with providing quality service to your customers. The fastest way to go into a tailspin after having had the sweet taste of success is to neglect your customers after the sale.

Giving Real Service, Not Lip Service

Gone are the days when a salesperson's service meant a slap on the back, a dirty joke, and belting down a few rounds of whiskey with the customer. Yet, oddly, many salespeople are still under the illusion that treating customers as "one of the boys" generates business.

As far as I'm concerned, it is not only unprofessional but ineffective. Lip service has nothing to do with real service, and it doesn't have a place in today's competitive business world. I have never told a dirty joke to a client; and I've never had a drink with one, either. And although I have picked up the tab for meals, those times had no resemblance to the entertaining of a customer. My conversations were strictly business, and every one of my clients knew that the only reason we were talking business during a meal was to conserve time.

When I call on my clients to service them, *I service them.* I am not in the entertaining business. The majority of my clients are very successful business and professional people; they, like me, place a high value on their time. They pay high premiums on the insurance I've sold them, with premiums sometimes running into the tens of thousands of dollars on multimillion-dollar policies. That's big business, and I think they deserve their money's worth. Being a stand-up comic and taking them out on the town is not my idea of service.

They can see better entertainment on television any night of the week, and they can afford to buy their own drinks and dinners at fancy restaurants. In fact, I think it borders on insulting customers if doing business means entertainment in lieu of good service. It sometimes can be construed as a form of a kickback. If so, it can backfire and actually cause you to lose the business. Some large corporations and government agencies prohibit employees from accepting any form of gratuity from any salesperson.

If you think that stopping in to kibitz with a customer will earn you "brownie points," you're way off base. We've all heard a salesperson say, "I was just in the area, so I thought I'd drop in." This doesn't build a good salesperson/customer relationship; it ruins one. First, the customer values his time and doesn't really want anybody to come in to interrupt him. In fact, if you do it too often, he'll warn his employees to tip him off—and make himself unavailable when you come around. Second, he'll think that if all you have to do is go around kibitzing with people, your time isn't very valuable—and he'll lose respect for you! When you analyze it, you have a lot more to lose than to gain by conducting business in this manner. *Give real service, not lip service.* That's what professional selling is all about.

Being a Goodwill Ambassador

I never forget that the success I've enjoyed during my sales career is due to the trust and confidence my clients put in me. For this reason, I always like to remind them how important they are to me. In addition to giving them complete product service, there are all kinds of little things I do to express my appreciation. First, as I mentioned earlier, every new client gets a thank-you-for-your-business letter. Several years ago, I began sending a walnut-engraved plaque to every customer who bought a million-dollar policy from me. On it was a favorite quote of mine by George Bernard Shaw: "You see things as they are, and you ask 'Why?' But I dream things that never were and I ask 'Why not?'"

When I started sending out these plaques, I was doing a lot of business with members of the National Association of Automobile Dealers. At their convention one year, there was a lot of talk among the dealers saying, "Did you get a plaque from Gandolfo? That's great! You must have bought a million too." It was as if they were members of an exclusive little club. It was my way of letting them know how much I appreciated their business.

Since I first started selling insurance, I began sending all of my clients birthday cards and Christmas cards. It's amazing how everyone appreciates getting a birthday card. Over the years, even some of the wealthiest and most sophisticated clients have commented to me how much getting my cards means to them. The average person receives only, at best, a handful of birthday cards each year; and I can't think of a single item that costs so little yet generates so much goodwill. I've had clients' children say to me, "Joe, you used to send me a birthday card after my father took out a policy on my life when I was a kid. I thought you were a member of our family. You hooked me as a client before I knew what insurance was."

Sending birthday cards isn't something that has to be confined to the insurance industry. No matter what you sell, find out your client's date of birth—and start mailing those cards. I guarantee you it will work like a charm!

I also make it a point to call each of my clients on the anniversary date of the sale. With all the changes that take place—not only in the insurance industry, but in all fields—it's important to conduct an annual review of their needs. In the insurance business, there are all sorts of changes happening, ranging from births to deaths in the family. I also send out questionnaires for my clients to complete, and this gives me some feedback on what their present needs may be. All of my clients receive a monthly tax letter from me, giving them updates on tax changes that might affect them. I'm also constantly sending copies of magazine and newspaper articles that I think may be of interest to certain individuals. I send a very nice Christmas present to my big clients; and likewise I send one to people who refer a lot of business my way, such as CPAs and attorneys. And again, anyone who gives me a referral, whether it results in a sale or not, gets a thank-you letter.

I think it's part of the job of *every* salesperson to serve as a goodwill ambassador to his customers. One large real-estate firm I know that sells approximately ten thousand homes every year has a special in-house employee follow-up on every sale and asks the buyer and seller if they were satisfied with the service the agent gave them. This broker teaches his agents to be thoughtful, too. For example, when a family is leaving the area after they have sold their house, agents frequently take them out to dinner or bring food over on the day when they are packing up to move. The agents in this firm always give the new home owners a thoughtful housewarming gift—something like a plant or a brass name tag to put on their front door. Other salespeople I know regularly send out "special-occasion cards" just to keep their names on the minds of their customers. These cards are cleverly written, usually containing a cute drawing or cartoon. They come in honor of a particular holiday such as Halloween, Thanksgiving, or Valentine's Day. If you want, you can find at least one holiday of some kind for every month of the year. I think these cards are a good idea; and for a low cost, they create a lot of goodwill.

A salesperson can do so many different kinds of goodwill things. The important thing is to develop an awareness for goodwill so that you will keep in constant touch with your customers. As a Halloween or Valentine card suggests, sometimes a salesperson has to *search* for a reason to keep his name on the minds of his customers. The important thing is that they know you care about them—you haven't forgotten them after the sale!

The Snowball Effect

Let the world know you for the service you give to your customers. I don't care what you sell—if you have devoted yourself to giving outstanding service to your clients, within two years, 80 percent of your sales will be either from referrals or repeat business. And as long as you continue in the business with this service-oriented attitude, you'll never have to worry about

being a top sales-producer. Check with any leading
salesperson and you will discover that satisfied clients
beget more satisfied clients. It is a snowball effect—
you build a solid core of customers around whom you
can build your career. And, each year, this nucleus
gets bigger and bigger. Unfortunately, most salespeople fail to recognize the importance of building
their careers around their existing clients; and in their
quest for new customers, fail to service the old ones
properly. Consequently, they get few referrals and little repeat business.

Service, service, service! Give your customers so
much service, they'll feel guilty *even thinking about doing business with somebody else.* Too often, customers
are abandoned after the sale; and this is a major mistake that, in the long run, not only shortchanges the
customer but the salesperson as well.

Never take your customer for granted. If you don't
give him the necessary service that he deserves, I can
assure you that not only won't you get referrals from
him, but you'll lose his business as well. In sales such as
copiers, word processors, and computers, the sale
doesn't end at the signing of the lease on the equipment. Leases don't automatically renew, and many are
month-to-month—which means that unless good service is given, the sale will go down the drain. In my
business, many agents think life insurance policies automatically renew year after year, generating years of
renewal commissions. These agents forget that insurance policies can lapse—and without servicing, they
will.

One real-estate broker told me that an agent can do
an outstanding job right through the closing; but some-

times just a minor detail, like not delivering the garage-door key, can upset the buyer and create irreparable ill will. The firm states that it takes just a handful of dissatisfied customers to ruin the company's reputation in a very short time. Needless to say, regardless of the cost of having a new garage-door key made and personally delivered by the agent, it's just good business.

Summing things up, one very successful salesperson told me, "I've worked very hard to establish a fine reputation, and today it's my number-one asset. But once this kind of reputation was obtained, it was up to me to work hard every day to keep it. I must continually prove myself."

If you're selling, you're in the service business!

Let me repeat: I don't care what you sell, you must be service-oriented. You can't give too much service! You first start providing service to your customer by communicating with him immediately *after* the sale. Make yourself available to him at all times. Don't become scarce after his money is in your pocket. Keep in constant contact with him. Let your world know you for your outstanding service. In the long run, your success will depend directly on your reputation.

11

Putting Your Act Together

Well, we've covered a lot of ground in ten short chapters. We dissected and inspected the anatomy of a sale, from the first attempt to get past a prospect's secretary to servicing your client after you close the sale. If you believe what I say in these pages and are adventurous enough to follow my suggestions, you could be on your way to earning more money than you ever thought possible. But there is still one hitch, one important factor that has to be mastered before all this information can be turned into a money-making machine. It's the reinforcement that keeps the chassis together, the oil that keeps the motor from burning out, and the fuel that will drive the machine to the goals you set for it. This miracle factor doesn't come from a book; it comes from deep inside of you. It's called *The Right Attitude* or *The Right Frame of Mind!*

The level of your performance—once you know what to do—is a good measure of your state of mind. I mean, your attitude or state of mind will make the difference between your becoming a very successful salesperson or just a mediocre one.

If you have a difficult time getting up in the morning, hating to face the challenges of the new day; if you tighten up at the thought of cold prospecting; if you feel a sense of relief when a potential customer doesn't answer the phone or is out when you arrive, you have a problem that has to be corrected. People who lack self-confidence often have a history of job-hopping, always hoping that a different product, a different customer, a different environment will change their lives. It rarely helps. Most people carry their weaknesses with them from job to job—usually blaming their problems on bad luck or the economy or anything but their own attitude.

Look, I know that it's not easy to go to work with a good, positive attitude if you have a history of falling short of the goals you have set for yourself. Nothing can bruise one's ego the way failure can. It's the proverbial vicious circle: failure breeds a destructive attitude and a bad attitude assures failure.

Recently I was approached by a real-estate agent I know; he was struggling to keep his head above water. He was a family man in his mid-thirties and had worked at five different sales jobs in the past six years.

"Joe, I'm thinking about quitting the real-estate business," he told me dejectedly.

"Why do you want to do that, Frank?" I asked.

"I just don't think there's much opportunity in it for me," he said in a low voice.

"Frank," I said, "in the past six years, you've sold for five different companies. First, it was insurance; then for a while you sold securities; and this is the third real-estate agency you've worked for in the past two years. What are you accomplishing by this?"

"I don't know, I just feel I *need* a change. Maybe to something like computers. Computers are really in now, Joe."

"I thought you liked the real-estate business?"

"Sure, I like it, but there's not much money in it right now, that's all. I need a change, Joe."

"Frank, let me tell you something," I said to him. "I see a pattern here. If you make a change now, there's a good chance you'll make another and another; and about thirty years from now, you will have gone through dozens of jobs. You know what? In the process, you will have wasted your life.

"I don't think it's the *work* that needs to be changed. And don't tell me that there's not any opportunity in real estate," I said, my voice rising a little. "It's ludicrous to say that. Both of us know many people who make a lot of money selling real estate. There's plenty of opportunity in the business—just as there was in selling insurance when you decided that you needed a change. And securities offered you a wonderful opportunity, but you never gave it a chance. The thing you've got to change is your mental attitude, not your job."

It's easy to say to someone, "Change your attitude," "Don't be afraid," "Get yourself into the right frame of mind," "*Shape up!*" But it's a lot easier said than done. It's hard to begin believing in someone who has let you down time after time—especially if that someone is you!

Since it's impossible to pull self-confidence out of the air, one must build self-confidence from the bottom up, from the inside out, a step at a time.

The giant step toward solving the attitude problem is admitting that you have one. There are dozens of symptoms, and we've touched on some: you can't get "up" for a presentation; you hate the paperwork and the travel and the hours; the people you have to sell are more like enemies than customers; people don't want you to succeed; others are luckier than you— they get the breaks, they're often favored over you; you're in a rut or a trap or the whole damned world has you backed against a wall; your spouse and kids don't appreciate you.

It's tough when your self-esteem starts melting away and your backbone turns into jelly. You need to succeed so much, and may be so afraid to fail, that you're frozen in your spot. If you move at all, it's often backward.

If you have an attitude problem, a self-confidence problem, a shattered-ego problem, *own up to it*. Make up your mind, once and for all, to face the problem and destroy it. Bring it to the surface of your consciousness—think about it. Find someone to talk to about it. Sometimes these problems are so deep-seated that one might need professional help: a job counselor, a clergyman, a shrink. Sometimes a spouse, a good friend, or a colleague can be helpful. The point is, you must not pretend the problem doesn't exist. You must look at it, analyze it, pick it apart. Most of your hang-ups are brought about by misperceptions and baseless fears. And like most boogeymen, they disappear when the lights are turned on. If you need help to find the light switch, get it as quickly as you can.

Attaining Self-Confidence—One Step at a Time

I remember how nervous I used to be as a young man when I had to speak in front of an audience. I'd actually get sick to my stomach. Back then, I never thought in a million years that I'd someday be a professional speaker addressing audiences all over the world. The key to my confidence level today is that I know what I'm talking about when I speak. I know my subject thoroughly. I am an expert—in front of an audience as well as across the desk from a prospect.

I wouldn't stand up in front of a large audience, however, and deliver an impromptu speech on something I knew nothing about. Nor would I deliver an impromptu sales presentation if I didn't know the product or the prospect. I have too fragile an ego to expose it to failure. Don't get me wrong—I'm not shy, but I'm not stupid either.

Self-confidence is attained by a series of successes; it comes one small success at a time. When I first started selling, I didn't go out and sell five- or ten-million-dollar life insurance policies as I do today. I started out selling small policies, five and ten thousand dollars apiece. In fact, I believed that it was so important for me to make at least one sale every day, there were times when I'd take *anything*—even an application for a thousand-dollar policy—just to know I had something at the end of every day. Back then, it was very important to me to have daily production—but the size of the orders didn't matter. What mattered was my knowing I had closed a sale. That knowledge helped build my self-confidence. It made me realize that if I saw people every day, the sales would automatically come. Soon I began to *expect* sales. I began to expect sales because I became *conditioned to closing sales every day!* Eventually, my little successes became bigger successes. I began to close those large sales just as easily as the little ones.

When I first started addressing audiences, I didn't speak in front of several thousands of people as I do today. My first speaking engagements were with small groups, usually five or six insurance agents in a local office. Again, it was only after speaking to small groups that the size of my audiences began to increase. Today, I feel comfortable addressing large audiences at conventions that sometimes number tens of thousands of people. I have also made many appearances on national television in front of millions of viewers, again always feeling at ease.

As a salesperson, you must set attainable, realistic goals; and gradually, as you reach them, stretch them a little further. If you set only long-term goals without establishing intermediate or short-term goals, they often appear to be so distant and even out of reach, causing you to become discouraged and to want to give up. I believe that a series of little victories in lieu of a long-drawn-out struggle for some grander but far-off objective is much more sensible—and in this way, long-term goals can be reached.

Once an ambitious young woman came to me asking for my guidance. She had just started a new career as a stockbroker. She told me, "In two years I plan to be the number-one salesperson for my company." While I admired her high ambitions, I didn't think she was taking a realistic approach. She had never sold anything in her life, and I knew it was going to take some time for her to establish herself—it's just not an overnight process to build a reputation in the securities industry so that wealthy clients entrust a neophyte with their funds.

While I didn't want to burst her bubble, I explained to her that it would be wise to establish some short-term goals first. "Why don't you set up some attainable goals, such as making a hundred calls every week on cold prospects," I recommended. "And aim to get five clients out of those calls. Now, if you get one new client a day, within a year you'll have two hundred and fifty. Then, while servicing those clients, keep right on making those cold calls; and at the same time try to average a minimum of one solid referral from each of your satisfied customers."

I went on to map out daily, weekly, monthly, quarterly, and annual goals for her to attain. It just didn't make much sense to have a long-term ambition without any short-term goals to make it all come true.

It's a basic rule that every human being learns as an infant. None of us suddenly stood up, walked, and then started running. Instead, we first learned how to crawl, then walk, taking one step at a time. As our parents praised us for taking that first step, we were encouraged to do better because *we gained confidence from that small success.* It's as the man replied when asked, "How do you eat an elephant?"

"One bite at a time" was his answer.

And finally, when you do set goals, have them be *your* goals. Don't allow anyone else to set them for you, such as your sales manager or boss. True success is accomplishing your own goals—not those that somebody else sets for you.

The Right Self-Image

You'll never look in the mirror and see a super salesperson looking back at you until you first see yourself as a super person.

"But, Joe," people say, "if I were successful, I'd have a good image of myself."

"You've got to have the right self-image *before* you're going to make it as a top-notch salesperson," I firmly insist. "And fortunately, if you don't have this image of yourself, there's a lot you can do to work on it."

As I have emphasized throughout this book, you've got to get yourself totally prepared. By doing your homework, you develop the confidence that lets you know you are an expert in your field. When you really know your business backward and forward, you have a wonderful feeling about yourself. Instead of running scared and fearing questions your prospect may ask about your product and company, you welcome them—knowing full well that you have the right information to satisfy all inquiries.

A good self-image also comes with time—after you have had many series of little successes. With enough of those little successes, you begin to *expect* bigger successes to happen. You anticipate success because you've become accustomed to it. For instance, when I walk into a prospect's office today, I know I am going to sell him a $5 million life insurance policy. I have had so many previous successes that I am conditioned to believe the sale will be automatic. All I have to do is give the presentation and I know I'll get the order. Now, my talking like this may sound cocky to some people, but that's what happens when you've had successes time and time again. It was all of those little five- and ten-thousand-dollar policies I sold during the early days of my career that gave me the self-confidence that I'd get the larger sales. I didn't start off expecting everyone to buy from me. It took time for me to develop my present-day self-image.

While some people frown on individuals like me who have strong self-images, I think it's a very positive thing. For instance, people sometimes remark that surgeons appear to be overconfident, sometimes too sure of themselves. But I think it's essential for a brain or heart surgeon to have this kind of self-image. When a surgeon is working under conditions that may require a split-second decision—one that means life or death to the patient—he had better have a wonderful self-image. The surgeon who doesn't is liable to be hesitant, and a slight quiver of the hand can be disastrous in the operating room.

Similarly, a salesperson must have the right self-image. As I told you in Chapters 8 and 9 on handling objections and closing the sale, you cannot project indecision. The way you visualize yourself is how your prospect will see you. It's something you can't hide. No matter what you say to him, your own self-image is projected in your voice, your eye contact, body language, and facial expressions. So, as you can see, you've got to have the right self-image. But it's not something that you can turn off and on. You must earn it by hard work and performance. Each little success paves the way toward other and bigger successes.

Imaging

Sometimes, before a tennis match, I meditate and mentally picture myself serving the ball. I'll focus on an image of my opponent returning the ball, and then I rush the net and put it away. I do it by simply shutting my eyes and "daydreaming" that I am playing tennis. It's incredible how much better I play a match when I've gone through this visualization before stepping onto the court.

Imaging is something I've always practiced in my sales career. When I first started selling, I'd constantly go through a mental exercise, always giving my sales presentation to prospects. I'd do it before shutting my eyes to sleep at night; and then when time would permit me, I'd pull over onto the side of the road while driving to appointments. Now, please note that imaging is more than simply saying the words and practicing the delivery of your sales presentation by saying it out loud. You've got to clear everything else out of your mind, and with your eyes shut, actually visualize a "real" sales interview. (For obvious reasons, you shouldn't do this exercise while driving.) Picture such things as making the telephone call and going through a complete telephone interview. Visualize the receptionist putting your call through, and then think about a warm reception your prospect will give you. Imagine yourself walking into an office. Picture yourself standing erect, shoulders back, head high, full of confidence. You're wearing your best suit, and you look and feel as if you own the place. You're busting with self-confidence because you're well prepared—and you know you're going to make the sale. Likewise, go through an entire sales presentation in your mind, always visualizing success. As I previously mentioned, you will develop the right self-image by attaining one success after another success. The successes that you attain during your imaging exercises also "count" and help you to develop that right self-image.

Our minds are our most powerful tools, enabling us to do wonders in preparing ourselves. I recall an interesting experiment with a class of schoolchildren who were tested for their accuracy in shooting foul shots on the basketball court. The class was split into three groups. The first group practiced shooting foul shots on the basketball court for thirty minutes every day for a month. The second group was instructed to sit at their desks for thirty minutes each day, close their eyes, and *imagine* themselves shooting foul shots. The third group did nothing. At the end of the month, all of the children were taken back to the court to be retested. While, understandably, the first group had improved greatly, *so had the second group!* No noticeable improvement, however, was recorded in the group of children who did nothing. And, just as these children's basketball skills improved who visualized themselves shooting baskets, so can you improve your selling skills.

The human mind has powers that enable us to do incredible things. In biofeedback, for example, a patient is hooked up to a device that feeds back information on his physiological processes. Then, the patient is monitored. A patient with tachycardia, a rapid heartbeat, can be hooked up to an oscilloscope, which gives a constant readout of the heartbeat. The patient is instructed to watch the monitor while attempting to relax. He is then told to form a mental picture of something very relaxing, such as himself in a hammock under a weeping willow tree on a lazy summer day. He imagines feeling a gentle breeze as he swings back and forth, thinking good thoughts and enjoying the beautiful day. As he does this mental exercise, a visual dis-

play immediately informs him that he is actually slow-
ing down his heartbeat. The biofeedback instrument
itself does nothing except tell him what is happening as
a result of his thinking.

As a way of illustrating the power that each of us
possesses, let me give you another example. O. Carl
Simonton and Stephanie Simonton, a world-renowned
oncologist/psychotherapist team, operate the Cancer
Counseling and Research Center in Dallas, Texas.
Much of their work is focused on cancer patients
whom they have instructed to do imagery exercises.
Many of their patients, who mentally picture healthy
white cells attacking and destroying cancer cells, have
been able to realize dramatic improvements in their
health. The Simontons' results in this area have been
impressive. Through these imagery techniques, some
patients, while also receiving medical treatment, have
actually been able to curtail and even cure themselves
of cancer! If dreaded cancer cells can be combated in
this manner, just think of the possibilities for im-
proving your selling skills and increasing your self-
confidence when you use imaging.

We all know that if practice doesn't make perfect,
at the very least it helps one to improve. So, in addition
to making actual presentations, through imaging you
enable yourself to get in additional practice. For instance, in the army, soldiers are trained to "dry-shoot"
on the rifle range. They first practice with an unloaded
rifle, slowly squeezing the trigger to avoid overanxiety
that may cause jerking. Once they've practiced many
times without ammunition, they actually begin shooting at targets—maintaining the same mental attitude,
going through the same calm, deliberate motions. I'm

sure the gunfighters from the Old West also practiced in a similar manner—before facing a real gunfighter for the first time. I don't suppose the ones who omitted this kind of practicing were around for a second gunfight!

Gentleman Jim Corbett, the great world heavyweight champion boxer, made the term *shadow-boxing* popular when he practiced his left jab in preparation for his big fight with the great John L. Sullivan. Corbett claims to have thrown tens of thousands of left-handed punches at his own image in a mirror before stepping into the ring with Sullivan—whom he defeated. Likewise, you can go through the same kind of mental exercise before you step into a prospect's office—your arena. As you do these imaginary presentations, your replies to rebuttals (your left jabs) and your mental alertness (being light on your feet) will improve. So will your reflexes and timing. Consequently, your imaginary sales will eventually become real ones!

How to Break a Selling Slump

At one time or another, every salesperson has a slump. Even if you do everything right, in the short run the theory of ratios can work against you—just as it works for you. I've seen many novice salespeople who start their careers like gangbusters; but as soon as they encounter their first slump, they can't cope with it and are knocked out of the business. I don't want this to happen to you, so let me tell you what to do when you have a slump.

First, you must recognize a slump for what it is.

Analyze why your production is down. Perhaps it's just a string of bad luck because the theory of ratios is working against you. For one reason or another, you might have called on prospects who were unqualified to buy your product. If so, you simply must make enough calls to *work* your way out of your slump. With enough calls, you're bound to run into more qualified prospects—and sales will follow.

Hard work is my best way to break out of a slump. I just let the theory of ratios resolve the problem. That's what I think is so great about selling. With enough calls, the numbers always make things right. What's more, when I'd be in a slump and make all those calls every day, I'd be so busy I didn't have time to think any negative thoughts. The people who remain in a permanent slump are the ones who don't work. They have a lot of time on their hands to think negative thoughts, and they don't produce anything positive to offset those negative thoughts.

I used to give myself daily goals; when I'd accomplish them, I would feel very good about myself. When I first started selling, I made it a point to sell a policy every day, no matter how small it was. I didn't care if it was just a few dollars' premium—I didn't like going home at the end of the day empty-handed. During my early days, I had some years when I averaged more than two sales every working day. For example, in 1969 I wrote policies on 724 lives for a total of approximately $33 million. That's an average sale of just over $45,000. The following year, my production was $63 million on 655 lives, so my average sale more than doubled. In 1971, I sold 526 policies for a total of

$114 million of life insurance. As you can see, I was really out there hustling and constantly selling policies on a daily basis.

One of my favorite ways to snap out of a slump is to reward and punish myself. Each day I used to set up small, attainable goals; and when I'd meet them, I'd give myself a present. My prize would be modest: perhaps I'd treat myself to a dessert, or I'd stay up an extra hour or maybe sleep in a little longer in the morning. I might even buy myself something such as a pair of tennis shorts or a new racket. I don't like people buying me birthday presents or Christmas presents, so I sometimes buy something luxurious—perhaps something as expensive as a new Mercedes. While many salespeople rely on incentives given to them by their sales managers, I always provided my own. By the same token, I'd punish myself when I was doing poorly. For instance, I'd sometimes fast for the next twenty-four-hour period because I did badly the previous day. I figured being mean and lean would sharpen me up!

Every salesman gets his share of rejection; that includes me. If you make enough calls, you're going to get turned down. Rejection is something that comes with the territory. However, any salesperson worth his salt can take it. As the saying goes, "No pain, no gain." Or as I like to put it, "No guts, no glory." And as Plutarch put it, "Those who aim at great deeds must also suffer greatly." If you want to hit home runs, you must understand that you'll also strike out a lot. Although Babe Ruth hit 714 home runs, he also struck out 1,330 times. And Thomas Edison, perhaps the world's all-time greatest inventor, recorded 25,000 failures in his attempt to invent a storage battery. When once interviewed about his work on the storage battery, the famous inventor said, "Those were not failures. I just learned twenty-five-thousand ways not to make a storage battery."

Now, I'm not implying that I'm not bothered by rejection. *I am, and so is everybody.* But I've learned to shake it off and go right on to my next call. You can't take it personally; and when somebody says no, always remember that they're not rejecting you—they just don't feel the need for your product. And as the theory of ratios tells us, "nobody sells 'em all." So the salespeople who see a lot of people are the ones who sell the most merchandise, though they may also get a lot of rejection. These salespeople also know, however, that there are only so many no's to be had out there; so each no means they are that much closer to a sale. With this in mind, they see a positive side to rejection—and it doesn't get them down.

If you're persistent, you will eventually come out of your selling slump with flying colors. Just don't allow yourself the luxury of feeling depressed and giving up. Here's a favorite illustration of mine that demonstrates persistence:

Failed in business in 1831
Defeated for Legislature in 1832
Second failure in business in 1833
Suffered nervous breakdown in 1836
Defeated for Speaker in 1838
Defeated for Elector in 1840
Defeated for Congress in 1843
Defeated for Congress in 1848

Defeated for Senate in 1855
Defeated for Vice-President in 1856
Defeated for Senate in 1858
Elected President of the United States in 1860—
Abraham Lincoln!

I've noticed that some salespeople become very discouraged following a bad day(s). They begin to question their ability, their product, and their company. Then they go out with their minds full of doubt and negative thoughts. They fear rejection as well as failure. As you can imagine, their problems become compounded. A bad day becomes a bad week; unless their attitude changes, they knock themselves right out of the business.

If your last call was a bummer, you must forget about it and go on to your next one. In a tennis match, you can't dwell on the last point you lost—there's nothing you can do about it. If you lose a football game, it's history. You learn from your mistakes and go out there to play your best in the next game. In one-to-one sports like professional tennis and boxing, every match has a winner, but there's also a loser. In golf and racing, there's only one winner out of a field of many. These professionals, who don't win every time out there, don't throw in the towel after suffering a defeat. Sure, they don't like it—I don't like it one bit either when I don't win—and neither should you. But you mustn't allow it to defeat you.

Take a .300 hitter in baseball, for example. Although he may become one of the major leagues' highest-paid players, he gets to first base only three times for every ten times at bat. Yet, imagine what would happen if he thought, "The odds are seven to three against me that I'll get a hit this time at bat." If a player had negative thoughts like that at the plate, he'd begin to move his hands, and his grip would change. His feet would move nervously, and his batting stance would change. He'd be thinking about not getting a hit, and by anticipating such a possibility, he would lose his concentration. Then he would have a difficult time keeping his eye on the ball. His timing would be thrown completely off. Not only would it be unlikely that he'd get a hit thinking this way, but if he continued, he'd go into a serious slump. Then watch his batting average take a nose dive.

Just as the baseball player has to *know* he's going to get a hit, so do you have to know you're going to make a sale. How you think will have a strong influence on how things work out. If you know you're going to make a sale, you probably won't be disappointed. On the other hand, if you know you won't get a sale, *you probably won't be disappointed either!*

Another way to break out of a selling slump is to go back and call on a satisfied customer. His enthusiasm will be good therapy; and while you're there you might pick up some good referrals who will be receptive, like your customer. I also recommend that you be around positive-type people and perhaps talk to some of your company's top salespeople or others in your community. Their enthusiasm will help restore yours. Each night you might also want to read some good books on motivation or perhaps listen to some inspirational tapes. Some of my favorite reading material is biographies of such men as George Patton, Harry Truman, Douglas MacArthur, "Bear" Bryant, Vince Lombardi, and John Wooden. I like to read some of the proverbs and psalms in the Bible. I like to watch movies such as *Brian's Song* and *Chariots of Fire*—these are the kinds of movies that make a guy want to run through the wall. They really charge you up!

Finally, as an effective remedy for breaking out of a slump, I recommend reviewing your product in great detail. Take a good look at the value you give your customer for his money, thinking in terms of his best interests. When your mind focuses on what you can do for the next guy without concern for yourself, things have a way of working out for you. Give to others, and I promise that it always comes back to you.

The Magic of Believing

In his book *Think and Grow Rich*, Napoleon Hill said, "Whatever the mind of man can conceive and believe, it can achieve." Those are words that I live by. Everyone needs a dream, and once you have yours, don't let anything but death itself interfere with it. And when you conceive your dream, believe in it so strongly that you will be filled with enough burning desire to attain it.

I've heard it said that success demands too high a price; and that in order to achieve a dream, many personal sacrifices are required and that, consequently, successful people are unhappy people. I don't buy that! I think people who fail to attain their dreams become discontent, bitter, and resentful. On the contrary, those people who succeed are content and caring. Success doesn't ruin people; failure does.

So go ahead and dream—and as you do, reach out

and attain your dreams. Then, as you do, keep right on raising your sights, always striving for higher plateaus. As Kahlil Gibran said, "The significance of a man is not in what he attains but rather in what he longs to attain."

When you consume yourself with a strong belief, everything you desire comes within your reach—if you're at peace with your God and have at least one person to share your success with.

In conclusion, you must remember that every great achievement got its start by being conceived in somebody's mind. Throughout this book I've given you the best selling techniques that guarantee proven results; but only by believing in yourself are they going to work.

So far, I've enjoyed a very successful sales career, and you can too. What's more, I don't believe there's anything I do that you can't do too. Everything I've told you in this book will work for anybody if you have enough desire. I haven't omitted any secret formulas—it's all right here. You just have to go out there and make it happen.

I wish you the best of everything, and may all of your dreams come true. God bless you.